P9-DOB-276

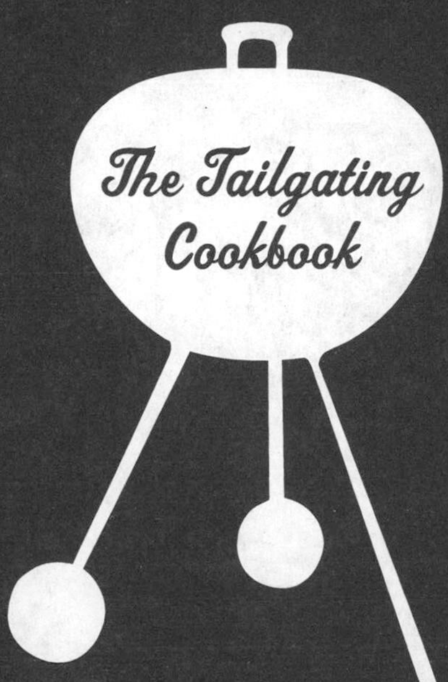
The Tailgating
Cookbook

BEER
CERVECERIA

The TAILGATING COOKBOOK

Recipes for the Big Game

★★★

by Bob Sloan

CHRONICLE BOOKS
SAN FRANCISCO

Library of Congress Cataloging-in-Publication Data available.

ISBN 0-8118-4605-9

Manufactured in Canada.

Designed by Jacob T. Gardner

Typesetting by Blue Friday

Cover photograph by Sheri Giblin

Distributed in Canada by Raincoast Books

9050 Shaughnessy Street

Vancouver, British Columbia V6P 6E5

10 9 8 7 6 5 4 3 2 1

Chronicle Books LLC

85 Second Street

San Francisco, California 94105

www.chroniclebooks.com

Acknowledgments

I'd like to thank the many people who willingly and colorfully shared their tailgating experiences with me: Mark and Annette Evans, Ben and Arlene Roth, Les Gutter, Warren Sexton, Barry Bauhmann, Craig Bauhmann, Molly Warner, Doug Guiling, Fred Olds, Deborah Stewart, Mark Gladstone, Mike Friedman, and Michael Repovich. Also everyone who helped to sample the recipes (some day I'd like to be one of those people): Phil and Sally Sanfield, Paul and Karen Izenberg, Lloyd Lynford, Suzie and Mario, Doug and Anne Stanton, the Obatas, the Warner-Kamslers, the Mintzes, Randi, Nate, and Leo. Props to Bill LeBlond and Amy Treadwell at Chronicle; shout outs to Josh Izenberg and to David Sanfield of Pitfire Pizza—The Crust you can Trust; and a toast to the tailgaters everywhere who are willing to put as much time and commitment into their food as their drink and enjoy themselves in a way that allows everyone tailgating around them to also have a good time.

CHARLES SHAW
80

Contents

INTRODUCTION

Back in the Good Old Days, most fans walked or took public transportation to the stadium. If they met for a beer before the game, they didn't call it tailgating. They called it "Hey, I'll meet you for a beer before the game." This took place at dingy bars in the shadow of the stadium—places with names like the Goal Post or the End Zone or Ralph's Stadium Tavern. The food, such as it was, might be a bag of chips, or a pickled pig's knuckle, or one of those eggs floating in a jar behind the bar that looked like a science experiment gone very, very bad. Later, during the game, there would be soggy hot dogs and stale peanuts at the park.

But one day all that changed.

Ah, to have been there at the moment of inspiration for the first tailgate party. It must have been a strange and mysterious vision, because the man pictured himself and his family and friends all dressed in the same color, arriving at the stadium hours before game time, lugging coolers full of food, pounds of bulky equipment, and bags of dripping ice to set up a party that could have been held so much more easily and comfortably in the backyard. What inspired him? Was it a voice, mysteriously calling to him from the parking lot? *If you grill it, they will come.* When he described to his wife what they were about to do, did she try to mask her concern behind a voice of reason? "Let's just eat here at home, Honey. Cooking the food—serving it—is so much easier. The bathroom is so much closer. And we have electricity!" But the voice, so clear in his head, called to him again, and he would answer her, "No, we won't eat at home. We will go to the parking lot and there we will set up a table and a barbecue grill and, dressed in our team colors, we will fill the air with the rich aroma of cooking meats. And soon others will be sure to join us. If we grill it, they will come!"

And come they did. By the millions. Once an anomaly confined to die-hard fans of college football, tailgating has become a routine sight at sporting events on every level, from the Little League World Series to the Super Bowl. Arena parking lots around the country are home to gatherings of all sizes serving every kind of food and drink. And those nontailgaters passing by, who, sadly, have come to the stadium only to watch the game, are quickly filled with envy when they see the platters of food. Many of them become instant converts, and at the very next home game they are out in the parking lot tailgating themselves.

Tailgate parties come in every size and shape. They can be as small as two buddies chowing down on homemade hoagies—along with a cooler of cold beer. They can be a van of happy fans scarfing homemade salsa and guac while cooking burgers or brats or chicken kabobs on a hibachi—along with a cooler of cold beer. Or they can be several generations of friends and family who have set up a field kitchen that would be the envy of many three-star New York restaurants and a network of tables laden with platters of meats, side dishes, and desserts—along with several coolers of cold beer.

Your tailgate party will no doubt fall somewhere along this continuum. And this book will provide you with what you need to know to devise a tailgating game plan and then execute it flawlessly.

GETTING STARTED

YOU KNOW YOU'RE A REAL TAILGATER WHEN

You forget the tickets but remember the ice.

★

Your memories of a crushing defeat center around a platter of dropped brats rather than the would-be winning touchdown pass dropped in the end zone.

★

You stop by the stadium on an off day just to gaze at your favorite parking space, fantasizing about where the team will put up the plaque in your honor and what it is likely to say.

★

You paint dividing lines like parking spots on your driveway and insist that your family eat on the blacktop at least once a week during the off-season.

★

You can't sleep the night after you discover that your neighbor has a portable blender more powerful than yours.

★

You can close your eyes and imagine a clear map of the location of the portable toilets in at least three different stadium parking lots.

★

You own one or more recordings featuring your team's marching band and/or highlights from radio broadcasts of their greatest games.

★

You have at least six beer mugs and a grill cover emblazoned with your team's logo.

★

You have tailgated at least once on one of the following occasions: child's birthday, Thanksgiving, New Year's Day, Valentine's Day, an anniversary of some consequence, Mother's Day.

★

You have canceled (or at least rescheduled) a round of golf because you realized it conflicted with a tailgate party.

If you answered yes to all of the above, it's clear that you already know what you're doing, and you can go directly to the recipes. If not, here are some guidelines on how to make yours a safe and successful tailgate party.

If you are about to embark on your first tailgate, you should think about going with a basic game plan. No end-arounds. No flea-flickers or halfback options. Your runs should be off-tackle, your passes short and to the sidelines. Choose a menu you feel comfortable with, a combination of do-ahead dishes and others that require only simple grilling. This will help reduce your anxiety once the tailgate starts. Another helpful tip is to pack all the equipment and utensils the night before, so in the morning all you need to think about is the food. And once you get to the parking lot, don't be intimidated by some of the more veteran tailgaters with their elaborate setups that resemble a small landing force. The first time they get to the majors, nervous minor league players remind themselves that the bases are still 90 feet away. In the same spirit, remind yourself that your grill will get just as hot as it does at home, the steaks will cook in the same amount of time, and they will taste every bit as good.

EQUIPMENT

Every season, it seems, new equipment and supplies are being designed especially for the avid tailgater. You can buy grills the size of a Sherman tank and smokers the size of whatever tank is the next size up from a Sherman. Gas-powered blenders not only add the option of blended drinks, but their roaring, lawn mower engines will help your friends find you in the vastness of the parking lot. Much of the new merchandise is for those who are in the advanced stages of

tailgating. I have always based my parties around a portable Weber charcoal grill, a few folding chairs, and a card table I got at a yard sale. I put my effort into the flavor of the food.

THE GRILLING EXPERIENCE

If you're planning to grill, you'll need a grill. Gas and charcoal work equally well. Charcoal grills can be much smaller, but even a hibachi, despite its diminutive size, can still crank out brats and burgers plus a few grilled shrimp kabobs. The recipes in this book assume that you will have either a gas or charcoal grill to use on-site (or a propane burner to heat up food that you have cooked at home). I strongly recommend having a chimney starter on hand to get the coals lit. They are very efficient and reliable. Charcoal lighting fluid has a bad smell, which might bother your neighbors, and it is less reliable. Electric starters require electricity, which you will probably not have. A grill-size bag of self-lighting charcoal also works well. Just remember to ignite self-lighting coals only in the recommended manner. No matter what method you use, keep a backup paper bag of about 2 dozen regular coals on hand to add to the fire in case it looks as though you'll lose the heat in the grill before getting everything cooked.

Tabletop Burner. Propane-fueled burners are an excellent supplement to a grill. They allow you to reheat dishes like chili or stew without taking up space on the grill. The burner will also keep pots of coffee, cider, or hot chocolate warm, which can be a good thing later in the season when the weather gets colder. These units are widely available, but look for those designed for portable kitchens rather than ones made for backpackers, which are smaller, produce less heat, and are more expensive.

Grill Safety. Choose a place to set the grill where it can't be easily bumped. Knocking into a pot of very hot chili can cause serious repercussions. Make sure you dispose of your hot coals properly. I douse mine several times with water, waiting until it stops sizzling completely. Too much water is better than stowing away a still-hot fire. Whatever you do, never hide a hot grill under your car or RV, thinking you will deal with the hot coals after the game.

Utensils. You worked most of the previous day shopping and prepping. You were up early doing the initial cooking. But all that hard work can be for naught if you are not properly prepared with bowls and platters to set out your wondrous creations, and plates and utensils for everyone to eat with. Make sure there is a platter or bowl for each dish. And don't forget the serving spoons. No one enjoys filling up their bowl of chili one plastic spoonful at a time.

THE FOLLOWING SHOULD BE IN YOUR TAILGATE KITCHEN SURVIVAL KIT

2 cutting boards

★

Chef's knife, serrated knife, paring knife

★

4 mixing bowls

★

Serving platters

★

Long-handled tongs and spatula for the grill

★

Several large spoons for stirring and serving

★

2 pots for reheating on the grill

★

Can opener, church key, and corkscrew

★

Lots of paper towels

Plastic bags—small for leftovers, large for garbage

★

Matches

★

Plates, bowls, and eating utensils

★

2 coolers—one for food, one for drinks and ice

★

2 large thermoses—one for coffee, one for hot chocolate or cider

Tables. Ideally you'll have at least two, one for food prep and another for serving. Tables also help define your space in the parking lot—the more tables you have, the more important and substantial your tailgate party must be. But most importantly, the table is where you set out your finished platters of food, putting into motion one of the essential tailgating pleasures—seeing the envy and jealousy in the less fortunate stadium-food-eating fans who walk by.

Chairs. Folding camp chairs are good to have around, even if you'll be sitting for the next three hours at the game. Tailgating can be tiring. Plus it's easier to eat sitting down. You may not need a chair for everyone, but have one each for tailgaters who are elderly, infirm, or are prone to imbibe too much.

Recreational gear. Throwing or kicking the appropriate ball around is part of the complete tailgate experience. It's also a good way to meet other tailgaters and get a little exercise before you confine yourself to the seemingly ever smaller space the stadium allots to you from which to view the game.

Sunscreen. Time goes quickly when you're having fun at a tailgate. And unless you're lucky enough to be set up in the shadow of the stadium, which, unless you're related to the team owner, is less than likely, there's a good chance you'll be tailgating in the sun. If you have a tent set up, this won't be an issue. But being exposed to the midday heat for three hours could result in some serious discomfort. Definitely consider wearing sunscreen. And a hat.

TAILGATING DEMEANOR

Those who have been tailgating in the same location for several seasons usually develop a community spirit. While you're more than likely to be welcomed into their midst (as long as you're wearing the home team's colors), you need to be mindful of tailgating decorum.

Be discreet. Don't play your music too loud—even if it is a recording of the school band. And don't let that touch football game get so raucous that you wind up throwing a long pass into someone's barbecue grill, which could ruin some very expensive steaks.

Both a borrower and a lender be. It's a given that everyone forgets something. Hopefully it won't be the porterhouse. Don't be afraid to ask a neighbor for what you may need. You might want to bring over a few wings as an offering. Maybe it will lead to an exchange of recipes. Maybe to marriage. By the same token, try your best to help out your fellow tailgaters. If you show up with any regularity, it's likely you will quickly become part of the local tailgating community. As a result, any kind deed will no doubt be returned many times over.

Loyalty. As anyone knows who has done it even once, tailgating is about more than just the eating. Displaying loyalty to your team, and sometimes your acrimonious feelings about the opposition, is essential. You may already have a collection of banners, hats, T-shirts, blankets, and other matériel required to make your allegiances clear. I've also provided opportunities to decorate a few dishes with your team's colors or, depending on your skill with cake

icing, the mascot. Observing the decorations of the more experienced tailgaters around you should give you some inspiration as to how you may want to adorn your area. Or you can try setting up your party in close proximity to a particularly demonstrative group and, by default, have some the manifestations of their devotion rub off on you.

FOOD

There is a contingent of serious tailgaters for whom tailgating cuisine consists of one of three things: brats, burgers, or both. Far be it from me to suggest that these die-hard fans change their ways. But if you are open to other flavors, to food in a shape other than a link or patty, if you are, so to speak, a tailgater willing to think outside the brat, then some wondrous opportunities await you. I have tried to create recipes that sparkle but do not require intensive preparation. Some have long ingredient lists, but this is not a reflection of their difficulty. While the food is an essential part of the tailgate experience, no one should be so distracted by the cooking that they can't enjoy themselves. These recipes balance flavor and prep time. That way no one is stuck cooking for the whole tailgate—unless, of course, they want to be.

All of the recipes identify which part of the preparation you will need to do at home and which at the tailgate. I have constructed them so that most of the hard work is done before you get to the party, so what is left is simple and straightforward.

The sides are all prepared at home and are brought to the party either ready to serve or needing only to be reheated or quickly cooked through.

The desserts need only be kept hidden until the end of the meal, at which point they can be served immediately.

LOCATION, LOCATION, LOCATION

At some stadiums, tailgating has become so popular that there's not enough room in the parking lot for people to park their cars. As a result, special areas (hopefully) near the stadium are reserved for tailgaters. You may need to call the stadium, racetrack, or team public relations office to find out what the deal is.

Bathrooms. Actual bathrooms are in the stadium. Portable ones ring the outside of the lot. Since tailgating often involves drinking a beer or two, unless you're in an RV, proximity to the nearest john should be a consideration. Each person knows how far he or she can walk when under the duress of having to go really, really badly. Your tailgate location should put you within that comfort zone. Other choices are to sport adult diapers or to bring your own Porta-John.

Neighbors. If you are a more demure type of fan, you may want to steer clear of bare-chested guys who have painted their faces and are performing ritual dances around a beer keg. You might instead look to situate yourself near some grandmother types setting out potato salad and pecan pies on checkered tablecloths.

TIMING

Arrival time at the parking lot depends on several variables:

How much cooking you have to do. If your menu requires grilling, you need to allow time to set up the grill, to get the coals hot, and to cook the food. You want to give yourself extra time to accomplish this, plus a few more minutes to borrow the things you neglected to pack. Hopefully, these are in the nature of ketchup or plastic cups and not the charcoal for the grill, which is considerably more embarrassing and potentially more difficult to scrounge up.

Availability of designated tailgating space. Certain stadiums have a more developed tailgating culture. At the most popular college games, like those at U of M and Ohio State, the spaces tend to fill up quickly. Ideally, you'll be brought to your first tailgate by someone experienced in the local tailgating scene. (There's a cottage industry waiting to blossom—Tailgate Consulting.) Even if you get to the parking lot early, you might discover you're in the spot someone's been tailgating faithfully in for several generations. Some serious college tailgaters I've spoken to pay an undergrad 8 bucks an hour to arrive at 6 A.M. in order to secure their favorite spot—a small price to pay to preserve a tradition—and the kid got to do some homework while he waited.

FOOD STORAGE

Safe storage is perhaps the most important component of tailgating. The maxim of food safety is "Cold food needs to stay cold and hot food needs to stay hot." Tailgaters mostly wrestle with the first part of this equation—how to keep the uncooked chicken, fish, meats, and dairy products cold from their refrigerator at home to the grill in the parking lot. A cooler with lots of freezer packs is the answer. You can layer the cooler with sections of newspaper to help divide the food and keep the cold packs localized. Keep in mind the maxim—it can't be too cold.

APPET

IZERS

You definitely want to serve a few appetizers at your party, even if it's just some bowls of salsa, guacamole, and Chex Mix. As the host, you will be busy getting the grill started, organizing the ingredients, and doing some last-minute prep, but the rest of your group is not so actively engaged. Once they've donned their team hats and painted their faces the team colors, they may want something to eat or drink. Or both. Without something to eat they might start acting ornery, the way they get when the umpire takes too long evaluating a replay in the last two minutes. Think about serving appetizers in two rounds:

THE FIRST ROUND

Have a few things prepared that are ready to go, like one of the salsas and chips, **Guacamole, Black Bean and Smoked Cheddar Dip, Deviled Eggs,** or the **Pecan Cheese Wafers.** You can get these out in an instant, since they are all ready to go, even employing someone else's organizational help while you focus on the rest of the meal. Having food out early will start the day off in a festive mood and help keep people from drinking on an empty stomach.

THE SECOND ROUND

These choices should be based on how you are cooking the main course. If your entrée requires serious grill time, serve an appetizer that requires no grilling at all, such as the **Cajun Wings, Classic Shrimp and Cocktail Sauce, Chicken and Chorizo Empanadas,** or **Pan-Seared Shrimp "Ceviche."** If your main course is a chili or stew and needs only reheating, you can afford to take some grill time for appetizers such as the **Grilled Tailgate Buffalo Wings, Beef Satay,** or **Korean-Style Spareribs.**

★ ★ ★

SALSA CRUDA

Serves 6 as an appetizer

You can find salsa at tailgate parties from U Mass to USC. This fresh salsa is best made the morning of the party. But since it's quick and easy, you'll still have time to check your team's Web site for the latest injury report.

6 Roma tomatoes, quartered lengthwise and seeded
1 red bell pepper, cored, seeded, and quartered
1 small red onion, quartered
¼ cup fresh cilantro leaves
1 clove garlic, chopped
1 teaspoon ground cumin
½ teaspoon cayenne
1 tablespoon olive oil
Salt
Tortilla chips for serving

At home Place the tomatoes, bell pepper, onion, cilantro, garlic, cumin, cayenne, olive oil, and 1 teaspoon of salt in the bowl of a food processor fitted with a steel blade and pulse until it is the equivalent of a medium dice. Be careful not to overprocess or the salsa will turn into a sauce.

Transfer to a sealable serving bowl and add more salt if needed. Refrigerate up to 8 hours.

At the tailgate Serve the salsa with tortilla chips.

Ocean Spray
4x4
igloo
HOT
COLD

ROASTED SALSA

Serves 8 as an appetizer

Roasting the vegetables gives this salsa a deeper, earthier flavor. It's a little more work than the fresh version, but the result is a more intense salsa. It will also last longer in the refrigerator, so you can make it a couple of days in advance.

- **3 tablespoons olive oil**
- **2 red bell peppers, cut in half lengthwise**
- **2 medium red onions, quartered**
- **10 Roma tomatoes, cut in half lengthwise**
- **2 jalapeño chiles, stemmed, seeded, and cut into quarters**
- **4 cloves garlic**
- **1 teaspoon chili powder**
- **1 teaspoon ground cumin**
- **1 teaspoon salt**
- **½ cup fresh cilantro leaves**
- **¼ cup fresh lime juice (from about 2 large limes)**
- **Tortilla chips for serving**

At home Preheat the broiler. Grease a baking sheet with 1 tablespoon of the olive oil. Lay the bell peppers and onions cut side down on the pan and dribble another tablespoon of the olive oil over them. Broil 4 inches from the heat until the peppers begin to char, about 12 minutes.

Remove the pan from the broiler and transfer the bell peppers to a brown paper bag. Close it and let them steam for 15 minutes. Transfer the onions to a platter.

Lay the tomatoes cut side down on the pan and broil them until they begin to brown on top, about 10 minutes. Remove from the broiler and let them cool.

Remove the bell peppers from the bag and peel off the charred skin. Also remove the seeds and stem pieces.

Transfer the bell peppers, onions, tomatoes, jalapeños, garlic, chili powder, cumin, and salt to the bowl of a food processor fitted with a steel blade and pulse until the mixture is the equivalent of a medium dice. Be careful not to overprocess or the salsa will turn into a sauce.

Place a medium skillet, preferably cast iron, over high heat, and let it get very hot, about 2 minutes. Add the remaining tablespoon of olive oil and spread it evenly over the pan. Add the salsa mixture and cook, stirring frequently, for 5 minutes.

Transfer to a sealable serving bowl and let cool. Stir in the cilantro and lime juice. Refrigerate for up to 2 days.

At the tailgate Serve the salsa with tortilla chips.

★ ★ ★

MANGO SALSA

Serves 8 as an appetizer

A lively and colorful alternative to tomato-based salsas, this goes well with grilled fish, but it's also great alone with chips. The yellow and black motif should also appeal to Steeler and LSU fans.

1 can (14 ounces) black beans, drained

2 mangoes, peeled, pitted, and finely diced

1 medium red onion, finely chopped

½ red bell pepper, cored, seeded, and finely chopped

6 scallions, green parts only, finely chopped

¼ cup fresh lime juice (from about 2 large limes)

¼ cup pineapple juice

½ cup chopped fresh cilantro

¼ cup chopped fresh mint

2 teaspoons ground cumin

1 teaspoon chili powder

½ jalapeño chile, stemmed, seeded, and finely chopped

Salt

Tortilla chips for serving

At home In a sealable serving bowl, mix together the black beans, mangoes, onion, bell pepper, scallions, lime juice, pineapple juice, cilantro, mint, cumin, chili powder, and jalapeño. Season with salt to taste. Refrigerate for up to 2 days.

At the tailgate Serve the salsa with tortilla chips.

GUACAMOLE

Serves 6 as an appetizer

Guacamole is one of those things people expect at a tailgate, like getting lost on the way back from a visit to the john.

- **2 Roma tomatoes, seeded and cut into ½-inch dice**
- **¼ cup chopped red onion**
- **¼ cup chopped fresh cilantro**
- **2 tablespoons finely chopped garlic**
- **2 ripe avocados**
- **¼ cup fresh lime juice (from about 2 large limes)**
- **Salt**
- **Tortilla chips for serving**

At home Assemble the tomatoes, onion, cilantro, and garlic in a sealable container and refrigerate until ready to pack.

At the tailgate Cut each avocado in half lengthwise, remove the pit, and scoop out the meat into a medium bowl. Mash the avocado with a potato masher or the back of a fork. Add the tomato mixture along with the lime juice and ½ teaspoon of salt and stir together until just combined. Add more salt if needed.

Serve immediately with tortilla chips.

Note If you'd rather make the guacamole entirely at home, lay plastic wrap directly over the surface of the guacamole, then cover the bowl and refrigerate for up to 8 hours.

CHEX MIX AND WASABI PEAS

Serves 6 as an appetizer

Everyone needs a recipe like this—something for which the ingredients can literally be picked up on the way to the stadium and then wantonly tossed together at the tailgate without any worry. It also has to be something people like, which is true of this combo. It's the wasabi peas that make it rock. They are available at most specialty food stores and health food stores.

1 box (9 ounces) Chex Mix
6 ounces wasabi peas

At home or at the tailgate In a sealable serving bowl, mix everything together with a clockwise motion.

PECAN CHEESE WAFERS

Makes 6 dozen wafers

Cheese wafers are one of those time-honored tailgate traditions that you think are outdated until you taste them.

- **½ cup (1 stick) butter, at room temperature**
- **2 cups grated sharp Cheddar cheese**
- **1½ cups unbleached all-purpose flour**
- **½ teaspoon salt**
- **½ teaspoon cayenne**
- **½ cup finely chopped pecans**

At home Using an electric mixer or a wooden spoon and some forearm strength (which will help you later off the tee), combine all of the ingredients in a large bowl to make a soft but not sticky dough.

Divide the dough into quarters and roll each piece into a log about 1 inch in diameter. Wrap each log separately in wax paper, and refrigerate until firm, at least 2 hours.

Preheat the oven to 350°F.

Unwrap the dough and cut it into slices about ¼ inch thick. Arrange the slices about ¼ inch apart on an ungreased baking sheet.

Bake the wafers until the edges are brown, about 18 minutes. Let them cool for 10 minutes on the pan before transferring them to a wire rack to cool completely. Store in a sealable plastic container for up to 1 week or freeze for up to 1 month.

At the tailgate Serve the wafers on a helmet-shaped platter.

★ ★ ★

BLACK-EYED PEA AND VELVEETA DIP

Serves 8 as an appetizer

I had to put in one recipe that used Velveeta. If it wasn't at the very first tailgate party, it was definitely there at the beginning. Even if it's not the most flavorful cheese, it will bring back memories and spark some conversation. "Velveeta? Is that still around?"

- **2 tablespoons olive oil**
- **1 medium onion, finely chopped**
- **2 cloves garlic, finely chopped**
- **1 can (15 ounces) black-eyed peas, drained**
- **8 ounces smoked sausage, cut into ¼-inch pieces**
- **½ cup purchased salsa**
- **¼ cup chopped fresh parsley**
- **1 teaspoon chili powder**
- **1 pound Velveeta cheese, cut into 1-inch cubes**
- **Fritos corn chips for serving**

At home Place a large skillet over medium-high heat and let it get hot, about 2 minutes. Add the olive oil and spread it evenly over the pan. Add the onion and cook until it gets soft, about 8 minutes. Add the garlic and cook for 1 minute more. Add the black-eyed peas, sausage, salsa, parsley, and chili powder and cook for 4 minutes more, stirring frequently. Add the Velveeta and continue cooking until it melts, about 2 minutes.

Transfer the mixture to a medium sealable bowl and mash with a potato masher until it is slightly smooth. Let the dip cool to room temperature. Refrigerate for up to 24 hours.

At the tailgate Let the dip return to room temperature before serving, preferably with Fritos.

★ ★ ★

BLACK BEAN AND SMOKED CHEDDAR DIP

Serves 8 to 10 as an appetizer

Cheese dips prevail in tailgate-land, each area of the country adding its own regional twist. I've seen or heard of beer cheese dip, Roquefort cheese dip, and pineapple cheese balls—all of which seem to me to require more courage than running a crossing pattern knowing Mike Singletary in his prime (which was pretty much his whole career) is just waiting for you in the middle of the field. This one features smoked Cheddar, which makes it less eccentric, but better.

- **1 can (15 ounces) black beans, drained, with liquid reserved**
- **½ red bell pepper, cored, seeded, and coarsely chopped**
- **½ small red onion, coarsely chopped**
- **4 scallions, green parts only, coarsely chopped**
- **½ teaspoon red wine vinegar or cider vinegar**
- **½ cup fresh cilantro leaves**
- **1 canned chipotle chile in adobo sauce**
- **1 teaspoon ground cumin**
- **1 teaspoon chili powder**
- **1 teaspoon salt**
- **1 cup grated smoked Cheddar or other smoked cheese**
- **Chopped chives for serving**
- **Crackers for serving**

At home Place the beans, bell pepper, onion, scallions, vinegar, cilantro, chipotle chile, cumin, chili powder, and salt in the bowl of a food processor fitted with a steel blade and process until the mixture becomes a smooth paste. Add some of the bean liquid if necessary to get the proper consistency.

Transfer the bean mixture to a medium mixing bowl and stir in the cheese.

Transfer to a sealable container and refrigerate until ready to pack.

At the tailgate Let the dip come to room temperature, then garnish with the chopped chives and serve with crackers.

★ ★ ★

CAJUN WINGS

Serves 6 as an appetizer

This is one of those dishes people will be asking for. Every week. It's what you will want to bring to your neighbors to thank them for lending you whatever it was you needed to borrow—even beer. It's what you should offer the people at the party nearby if you are romantically inclined and you want to make a good impression. But be warned, no matter how many of these wings you make, it won't be enough.

3 pounds chicken wings, tips removed
3 tablespoons olive oil
3 tablespoons fresh lemon or lime juice
3 tablespoons brandy, tequila, or rum
1 tablespoon Dijon mustard
1 tablespoon sweet paprika
2 teaspoons dried thyme
2 teaspoons ground cumin
2 teaspoons ground coriander
2 teaspoons caraway seeds
4 cloves garlic, finely chopped
½ teaspoon cayenne
1 teaspoon salt
1 lemon cut in half crosswise
Hot sauce for serving

At home Simmer the chicken wings in just-boiling water for 8 minutes, then drain and set aside to cool. Preheat the oven to 375°F.

Put the olive oil, lemon juice, brandy, mustard, paprika, thyme, cumin, coriander, caraway seeds, garlic, cayenne, and salt in a blender and pulse a few times until it becomes a medium-thick paste. Transfer the wings to a large bowl, add the sauce, and toss so the wings are entirely covered. Arrange them in a single layer on a baking pan and bake, uncovered, on the center rack until the skin turns deep brown and is quite crisp, about 35 minutes.

During the last 15 minutes, find a place on the baking pan for the 2 lemon halves, cut side down. Let the wings cool, then store them along with the lemon halves in a sealable container and refrigerate, unless you are packing to leave.

At the tailgate Let the wings come to room temperature. Before serving, squeeze the lemon halves over the wings, along with a few dashes of hot sauce.

Note Chicken wings come in 3 pieces. I always cut off the tip and usually leave the remaining two sections together, which makes cooking them slightly more expedient. However, when I can, I buy the packages of "drumettes," which is the meatiest section of the wing. Usually I stock up when I find them and freeze some for future games.

GRILLED TAILGATE BUFFALO WINGS

Serves 6 to 8 as an appetizer

Buffalo wings originated at the Anchor Bar in Buffalo, where, on October 30, 1964, legend has it that owner Teressa Bellissimo was stuck feeding her son and his friends a late-night snack. Most normal parents would politely say, "What do I look like I'm running here—an all-night diner?" But since Teressa was, in fact, running something much like an all-night diner, she fried up some chicken wings (the cheapest item in the walk-in, mind you), smothered them in a spicy sauce, and served them with celery sticks and blue cheese dressing to cut the heat. With this one impulsive act, Teressa set a bad parental precedent but created the legendary Buffalo wing. Unlike Teressa's wings, tailgate wings are grilled, not fried.

3 pounds chicken wings, tips removed
3 tablespoons olive oil
2 teaspoons salt
¼ cup (½ stick) margarine
3 tablespoons Louisiana hot sauce
1 tablespoon white vinegar
⅛ teaspoon celery seed
¼ teaspoon cayenne
1 teaspoon garlic powder
Dash of ground black pepper
¼ teaspoon Worcestershire sauce
Blue cheese or ranch dressing for serving

At home Place the wings in a large bowl, add the olive oil and salt, and toss so they are lightly coated. Transfer to a sealable container and refrigerate until you are ready to pack.

In a separate sealable container, assemble the margarine, hot sauce, vinegar, celery seed, cayenne, garlic powder, black pepper, and Worcestershire sauce and refrigerate until you are ready to pack.

At the tailgate Prepare coals for a medium-hot fire.

While the coals are heating, transfer the ingredients for the sauce into a small saucepan.

When the coals are ready, grill the wings, turning them every 6 minutes or so, until they are crispy and cooked through, about 30 minutes.

During the last 10 minutes of cooking, place the saucepan on the grill and heat it until the margarine melts and the sauce is heated through, for about 30 minutes.

Transfer the wings to a platter, stir the sauce well, and pour it over the wings. Serve accompanied by your favorite dressing.

TAILGATING TALES

MEMORIES OF DAD AND DEVILED EGGS

My friend Molly remembers her mom packing up an egg carton with a dozen of her special deviled eggs before the family loaded into their '62 Country Squire to tailgate before a University of Minnesota football game. As her dad had once played for the Gophers, their table became a gathering place for fans and former players who wanted to reminisce about seasons past. The tailgate party was where she got a chance to bask in her dad's former glory as teammates and fans dropped by to pay their compliments. There was a lot of hand-shaking and backslapping as they remembered some great play he'd made, though Molly suspected the valiance of her dad's effort might have gradually escalated over the years. Still, it was on those chilly afternoons that her dad's former life as a college player came alive to her in ways that the photos in his college yearbook never could.

★ ★ ★

DEVILED EGGS

Makes 24 eggs

One of the interesting aspects of the institution of tailgating is its role in preserving classic American recipes that otherwise might go on the endangered list. Like deviled eggs. You won't read about them in any of the gourmet cooking magazines. And I'll bet that even church picnics are now featuring wraps and Caesar salads. But in the parking lot, deviled eggs are alive and well, as they have been for many years.

12 eggs
¼ cup mayonnaise
1 tablespoon Dijon mustard
Salt and ground black pepper

At home Fill a large bowl halfway with cold water and dump in a tray of ice cubes.

Place the eggs gently in a pot of cold water and bring to a boil over medium-high heat. Reduce the heat to medium-low and simmer the eggs for 10 minutes. Remove them with a slotted spoon and plunge them into the bowl of ice water.

Peel the eggs and cut them in half lengthwise. Remove the yolks and transfer them to a medium mixing bowl. Add the mayonnaise and mustard and salt and pepper to taste and mash together.

Spoon the yolk mixture back into the egg whites. Arrange the eggs in the egg carton to transport to the tailgate. Refrigerate until ready to pack. (You will need an extra empty egg carton, which you hopefully have saved for this purpose. If not, ask your neighbor—and if you have an extra ticket, invite her along.)

Variations **Deviled Eggs with Bacon:** Crumble 6 pieces of cooked bacon and add them to the egg yolk mixture, along with 1 finely chopped jalapeño and 2 finely chopped scallions, green parts only.

Deviled Eggs with Crabmeat: Fold 8 ounces lump crabmeat, 1 tablespoon chopped fresh parsley, and 1 teaspoon lemon juice into the egg yolk mixture.

Deviled Eggs with Ham and Capers: Fold 2 ounces chopped ham and 1 tablespoon chopped capers into the egg yolk mixture.

CLASSIC SHRIMP AND COCKTAIL SAUCE

Serves 6 as an appetizer

Like Marino to McDuffie or Montana to Rice, shrimp and cocktail sauce is a winning combination. Shrimp is also a great way to keep any tailgate festive, even if you are a Philadelphia Eagles fan about to enter the post-season and a sense of impending doom has already descended on the Vet parking lot.

SHRIMP

1½ pounds large shrimp
¼ cup Old Bay seasoning
½ cup fresh lemon juice (from about 3 medium lemons), reserving the juiced lemons

COCKTAIL SAUCE

¾ cup ketchup
3 tablespoons prepared horseradish, or to taste
2 tablespoons fresh lemon juice
1 teaspoon chili powder
1 teaspoon garlic powder
Romaine or Boston lettuce leaves for garnish

At home **For the shrimp:** Peel and devein the shrimp, leaving the tail on if you want. (The shrimp won't care.) Refrigerate.

Combine 6 quarts of water with the Old Bay seasoning, lemon juice, and juiced lemons in a large pot and bring to a boil. While the water is heating, arrange a baking sheet on a wire rack. When the water comes to a boil, add the shrimp and cook until they are opaque and cooked through, 4 to 5 minutes. Immediately drain the shrimp in a colander and transfer them to the baking sheet. Let the shrimp cool, then transfer to a sealable container and refrigerate until you are ready to pack.

For the cocktail sauce: Place the ketchup, horseradish, lemon juice, chili powder, and garlic powder in a medium bowl and mix together until well combined. You can use more or less horseradish, depending on your taste. Transfer to a sealable container and refrigerate until you are ready to pack.

At the tailgate To serve, line a serving platter with lettuce leaves and arrange the shrimp over them. Put a small bowl or one of those mini helmets they serve the ice cream in at the stadium in the center, and fill it with the sauce.

Note When transporting the shrimp, line the bottom of the container with several layers of paper towels to absorb the liquid the shrimp tend to exude.

LOBSTER ROLLS

Makes 6 sandwiches

In terms of cost and labor, these sandwiches are at the other end of the tailgating spectrum from a grilled brat in a bun. But before you deem this dish too posh for the parking lot, try it once and see what your crowd is talking about the next time you tailgate.

3 live lobsters (1¼ pounds each)
½ cup finely chopped celery
½ cup finely chopped red onion
2 tablespoons mayonnaise
2 tablespoons sour cream
1 tablespoon fresh lemon juice
½ teaspoon salt
6 hot dog buns

At home Cook the lobsters for 8 minutes in enough boiling water to cover them. Transfer to a large bowl and let them cool. While the lobsters are cooling, stir together the celery, onion, mayonnaise, sour cream, lemon juice, and salt in a medium bowl and set aside.

When the lobster has cooled, remove the meat from the tail and claws and chop into ½-inch pieces. Place the lobster meat in the bowl with the dressing and stir to combine. Transfer to a sealable container and refrigerate until you are ready to pack.

At the tailgate Fill each bun with lobster salad and serve.

Note If you still have more cooking to do, do not turn your back on the platter of lobster rolls. When you turn around again, they will be gone.

12
OPENING DAY
NFL

★ ★ ★

PAN-SEARED SHRIMP "CEVICHE"

Serves 6 as an appetizer

Not a true ceviche, since the shrimp are cooked first, but I'm hoping this small inconsistency won't bother you. It's an awesomely refreshing and flavorful dish to serve on a hot day.

½ cup purchased tomatillo salsa
1 cup fresh cilantro leaves
4 cloves garlic
4 tablespoons olive oil
2 teaspoons ground cumin
1 teaspoon chili powder
1 teaspoon salt, plus more for seasoning
¼ teaspoon cayenne
3 pounds large shrimp, peeled and deveined
¼ cup fresh lime juice (from about 2 large limes)
2 tablespoons fresh orange juice
1 tomato, cored, seeded, and cut into ¼-inch dice
2 scallions, green parts only, finely chopped
¼ cup finely chopped red onion
Ground black pepper

At home Put the tomatillo salsa, ½ cup of the cilantro, the garlic, 2 tablespoons of the olive oil, the cumin, chili powder, the 1 teaspoon salt, and the cayenne in the bowl of a blender and pulse until it is just puréed. Pour half of the marinade over the shrimp and refrigerate for 1 hour. Reserve the remaining half.

Place a large skillet over high heat, and let it get very hot, about 2 minutes. Add 1 tablespoon of the olive oil and spread it evenly over the pan. Add half the shrimp and cook, stirring frequently, until they are opaque in the center, about 5 minutes. Wipe out the pan and return it to the heat. Add the remaining tablespoon olive oil and repeat with the rest of the shrimp.

Coarsely chop the remaining ½ cup cilantro and transfer to a medium bowl along with the reserved marinade. Add the lime juice, orange juice, tomato, scallions, and onion and mix together. Add the cooled shrimp and toss to coat. Season to taste with salt and pepper. Transfer to a sealable container and refrigerate until you are ready to pack, up to 4 hours.

At the tailgate Serve the shrimp cold in a large bowl, setting out some small plates and forks for your guests to eat with.

CHICKEN AND SAUSAGE QUESADILLAS

Serves 8 as an appetizer

Quesadillas are a natural for tailgating. They come all wrapped up and ready to put on the grill, like a present from the tailgating gods.

- **2 tablespoons vegetable oil**
- **6 skinless, boneless chicken thighs, cut into small pieces**
- **8 ounces andouille or other smoked, spicy sausage, crumbled or cut into ½-inch pieces**
- **1 red bell pepper, cored, seeded, and finely chopped**
- **1 medium onion, finely chopped**
- **4 cloves garlic, finely chopped**
- **1 can (4 ounces) diced green chiles, drained**
- **1 jalapeño chile, stemmed, seeded, and finely chopped**
- **1 tablespoon chili powder**
- **1 teaspoon ground cumin**
- **½ teaspoon salt**
- **8 flour tortillas, quesadilla size**
- **2 cups grated Cheddar cheese**

At home Place a large skillet, preferably cast iron, over high heat, and let it get very hot, about 2 minutes. Add the vegetable oil and spread it evenly over the pan. Add the chicken, sausage, bell pepper, and onion and cook until the chicken is cooked through and the vegetables soften, about 8 minutes. Add the garlic, green chiles, and jalapeño and cook for 2 minutes more. Add the chili powder, cumin, and salt and cook for 1 minute more, stirring continuously.

Transfer to a bowl and let cool completely, or refrigerate for up to 24 hours.

Lay a tortilla over a 16-inch-long piece of aluminum foil. Spread one-fourth of the cooled chicken mixture evenly over the tortilla. Top with one-fourth of the cheese. Lay a second tortilla on top of the cheese and press down gently. Wrap the quesadilla in foil and repeat. Pack the wrapped quesadillas in a container and refrigerate until you are ready to pack. Keep them flat while transporting them.

At the tailgate Prepare coals for a medium fire. When the coals are ready, lay the quesadilla packages on the grill and cook for 3 minutes. Turn and cook for 3 minutes more.

Remove the quesadillas from the foil and lay each one on the grill. Cook until they begin to get some grill marks, about 1 minute. Turn and cook for 1 minute more.

Cut each quesadilla into 8 pieces (this is most easily done with scissors) and serve.

Note You can replace the chicken and/or sausage with equal amounts of leftover cooked steak, pork, hamburger, or fish. Or leave the meat out altogether and add some slices of roasted red pepper and artichokes for great veggie quesadillas.

CHICKEN AND CHORIZO EMPANADAS

Serves 10 to 12 as an appetizer

I feel as much pride making these empanadas as I do any other dish. I've brought these to tailgates with some serious steak-and-then-more-steak Giants fans. And I've served them to svelte Upper East Side ladies in the park before one of my kids' soccer games. Everyone is equally knocked out by them. Be sure to let the filling cool completely before assembling the empanadas; otherwise the pastry will fall apart. It's actually best to make both the filling and pastry the day before and then refrigerate them overnight. This makes the ritual "Filling of the Empanadas" go a lot easier. Ring the outside of the grill with empanadas to reheat them. Serve as a first course, as a main course, as the only course.

DOUGH

- 2 cups unbleached all-purpose flour
- 2 cups masa harina (see note)
- ½ cup grated Cheddar cheese
- ¼ cup sugar
- 1 teaspoon baking powder
- 2 teaspoons salt
- 1 egg
- ¾ cup (1½ sticks) butter, melted and cooled slightly
- 1 cup water, plus more as needed

FILLING

- 2 tablespoons vegetable oil
- 8 ounces chorizo, cut into small pieces
- ½ cup finely chopped onion
- 1 pound ground chicken or turkey
- ½ cup coarsely chopped pitted green olives
- ½ cup golden raisins
- 3 tablespoons finely chopped garlic
- 1 tablespoon chili powder
- 1½ teaspoons ground cumin
- ½ cup chicken broth

- 1 egg
- 2 tablespoons water

At home **For the dough:** Measure the flour, masa harina, cheese, sugar, baking powder, and salt into a large bowl and whisk together. Make a well in the center, add the egg and the melted butter, and stir to incorporate them.

Add the 1 cup water and stir until the dough begins to hold together. Add more water if needed, a tablespoon at a time, until you have a soft, pliant, nonsticky dough.

Knead the dough a few times, then divide it in half and shape each into a ball. Wrap each ball with plastic and refrigerate for at least 2 hours and up to 48 hours.

For the filling: Place a large skillet over high heat and let it get very hot, about 2 minutes. Add 1 tablespoon of the vegetable oil and spread it evenly over the pan. Add the chorizo and cook until it is cooked through and no longer pink, about 6 minutes. Transfer the chorizo to a medium bowl with a slotted spoon and pour out any excess grease from the pan.

Add the remaining tablespoon vegetable oil to the skillet along with the onion and cook until it begins to soften, about 4 minutes. Add the chicken and cook until it is cooked through and loses its pinkness, about 8 minutes, breaking up the clumps of meat with the back of a spoon.

Add the olives, raisins, garlic, chili powder, cumin, and chicken broth and stir to combine. Bring the liquid to a boil, then reduce the heat to low and simmer, stirring frequently, until the liquid is almost gone, about 12 minutes. Transfer to a bowl and chill for at least 4 hours or overnight.

Preheat the oven to 350°F. In a small bowl, whisk together the egg and water to make an egg wash.

Lightly flour a work surface. Start flattening one of the chilled dough balls with your palms, then roll the dough out until it is about ¼ inch thick.

Use a 4-inch cookie cutter or the top of an empty can to cut the dough into circles. Gather up the remaining dough scraps and set aside.

Brush the egg wash in a ½-inch border around the outer edge of each circle of dough. Place a tablespoon of filling in the center of each circle. Fold the dough to create a half-moon-shaped pastry. Crimp the edges together by gently pressing them with the tines of a fork. Use the fork to poke 2 sets of holes in the top.

Place the finished empanadas on an ungreased baking sheet and brush the top with the egg wash. You can pack them close, but make sure they aren't touching. Repeat with the remaining dough.

Bake on the center rack of the oven until lightly browned on top, 35 to 40 minutes. Transfer to a wire rack and let cool. Refrigerate until ready to pack.

At the tailgate Serve the empanadas at room temperature or reheat them around the edge of the grill for 2 minutes on each side.

Note Masa harina is made from corn, but it is different from cornmeal. It can be found in most specialty food shops and definitely in any Hispanic market.

★ ★ ★

KOREAN-STYLE SPARERIBS

Serves 6 to 8 as an appetizer

These are a definite choice to make when your team is having a losing season, because no matter how bad things are–missed extra points, fumbles inside the 1-yard line, a whole game of three-and-outs–these ribs will lighten your spirits and make the world seem a far more forgiving place.

2	**racks spareribs, trimmed**
1½	**cups white wine**
¾	**cup soy sauce**
1	**bunch scallions, green parts only, finely chopped**
3-inch	**piece fresh ginger, peeled and finely chopped**
8	**cloves garlic, coarsely chopped**
6	**tablespoons brown sugar**
1	**tablespoon Chinese five-spice powder**

At home Cut each rack into individual ribs. Place them in a large pot and add the wine, soy sauce, scallions, ginger, garlic, brown sugar, and five-spice powder. Bring to a boil, cover, reduce the heat to low, and simmer for 1 hour. Remove the pot from the heat and let the ribs cool in the cooking liquid.

Transfer the ribs with a slotted spoon to a sealable container. Skim the fat from the cooking liquid and pour the skimmed liquid over the ribs. Refrigerate until you are ready to pack, up to 24 hours.

At the tailgate To finish the ribs, prepare coals for a medium fire. When the coals are ready, arrange the ribs on the grill so they aren't touching. Grill for 12 minutes, turning several times and basting each time with the sauce. Serve immediately.

TOYOTA

★ ★ ★

GRILLED SHRIMP TACOS

Makes 16 tacos

I like the smoky heat of the chipotle married with the sweet flavor of the mango. It's a Mars/Venus thing, but it works. The short grilling time means you can punch out a few skewers of shrimp and still have plenty of heat left in the coals to cook some steaks or burgers while everyone else is savoring the tacos. Just make sure someone saves you one.

- **2 ripe mangoes**
- **2 canned chipotle chiles in adobo sauce, finely chopped**
- **2 tablespoons adobo sauce from the chipotle chiles**
- **1 cup purchased medium-spicy salsa**
- **½ cup diced red onion**
- **½ cup diced red bell pepper**
- **4 scallions, green parts only, finely chopped**
- **¼ cup finely chopped fresh cilantro**
- **½ cup fresh lime juice (from about 3 large limes)**
- **Salt**
- **2 pounds large shrimp**
- **¼ cup olive oil**
- **Ground black pepper**
- **16 corn tortillas**
- **Shredded lettuce for serving**
- **2 limes, quartered**

At home Cut the mangoes lengthwise along both sides of the pit. Use a spoon to scoop out the flesh and then chop it into medium dice. Transfer to a medium mixing bowl along with the chipotle chiles, adobo sauce, salsa, onion, bell pepper, scallions, cilantro, lime juice, and salt to taste and stir together. Transfer to a sealable container and refrigerate until you are ready to pack, up to 4 hours.

Peel and devein the shrimp. Thread the shrimp onto skewers, making sure not to crowd them. Brush both sides with the olive oil and sprinkle with salt and pepper. Transfer to a sealable container and refrigerate until you are ready to pack, up to 4 hours.

At the tailgate Prepare coals for a medium-hot fire. When the coals are ready, grill the shrimp, turning once, until they are opaque in the center, 6 to 7 minutes. Transfer to a serving bowl.

Heat the tortillas briefly on the grill until they soften, about 30 seconds on each side. Stack them on a plate and cover with a clean kitchen cloth.

To serve, place the bowl of shrimp on your serving table along with the tortillas, mango mixture, shredded lettuce, and limes. Have your guests assemble their own tacos by filling each tortilla with a few shrimp and then topping them with a few generous spoonfuls of the mango mixture and some shredded lettuce. Squeeze fresh lime juice over the filling, then fold and eat.

Note If using wooden skewers, soak them in water for 1 hour before using to keep them from burning during grilling.

★ ★ ★

BEEF SATAY

Serves 6 to 8 as an appetizer

Not the artfully shaped sliver of meat that you might be offered at a gallery opening. Not a miniature swatch of sirloin, like you might see at the free "Meet Your Shipmates" buffet the first night of a cruise. But an ample, butch piece of tasty grilled beef on a stick—like what you might find at a tailgate party.

¼ cup soy sauce
¼ cup fresh orange juice
¼ cup white wine
¼ cup Thai fish sauce
4 cloves garlic, finely chopped
2 tablespoons fresh lime juice
2 tablespoons finely chopped fresh ginger
1 teaspoon ground cumin
1 teaspoon ground coriander
1 tablespoon "natural" peanut butter
1 tablespoon brown sugar
1 flank steak (about 1 pound), cut crosswise at an angle into ¾-inch strips

At home In a medium bowl, mix together the soy sauce, orange juice, wine, fish sauce, garlic, lime juice, ginger, cumin, coriander, peanut butter, and brown sugar.

Thread a slice of steak onto a skewer, weaving it back and forth several times so the meat is not flopping and is close to the stick. Place the skewers in a sealable container just big enough to hold them. Pour the marinade over them and make sure the meat is coated on all sides. Refrigerate until you are ready to pack, at least 1 hour and up to 6 hours.

At the tailgate Prepare coals for a hot fire. When the coals are ready, grill the beef for 6 to 7 minutes, turning once and brushing with the remaining sauce, for medium-rare. Serve immediately.

Note If using wooden skewers, soak them in water for 1 hour before using to keep them from burning during grilling.

★ ★ ★

TUNA WITH SWEET AND SPICY SAUCE

Serves 6 as an appetizer

This is a special, rather refined first course that, even though it is quite easy to prepare, is unexpected in the parking lot. It's probably not what the offensive linemen are eating after the game. Maybe the place kicker. Actually, maybe the place kicker's wife.

1-pound piece sushi-grade tuna
½ cup olive oil
2 tablespoons dark (Asian) sesame oil
¼ cup soy sauce
¼ cup fresh orange juice
2 tablespoons honey
2 tablespoons chopped fresh ginger
2 tablespoons chopped garlic
½ teaspoon cayenne
½ teaspoon curry powder
2 scallions, green parts only, finely chopped
Sesame seeds for garnish

At home One hour before leaving, place the tuna in a sealable container just large enough to hold it. Pour the olive oil and sesame oil over it and refrigerate.

In a small pot, mix together the soy sauce, orange juice, honey, ginger, garlic, cayenne, and curry powder and bring to a boil. Immediately reduce the heat to low and simmer for 5 minutes. Strain the sauce into a bowl, then transfer to a sealable container and refrigerate until you are ready to pack, up to 24 hours.

At the tailgate Prepare coals for a hot fire. When the coals are ready, transfer the tuna directly to the grill (do not pat dry) and cook for 5 to 6 minutes, turning once, for medium-rare.

Let the tuna cool for 10 minutes, then cut it into ½-inch slices. Arrange the slices on a plate and dribble the sauce over them. Sprinkle with the chopped scallions and sesame seeds.

Eat with chopsticks, plastic forks, or your fingers.

Note The only real trick to this dish is keeping the tuna cold on the way to the game. Place it in the freezer ½ hour before traveling to keep it extra-fresh.

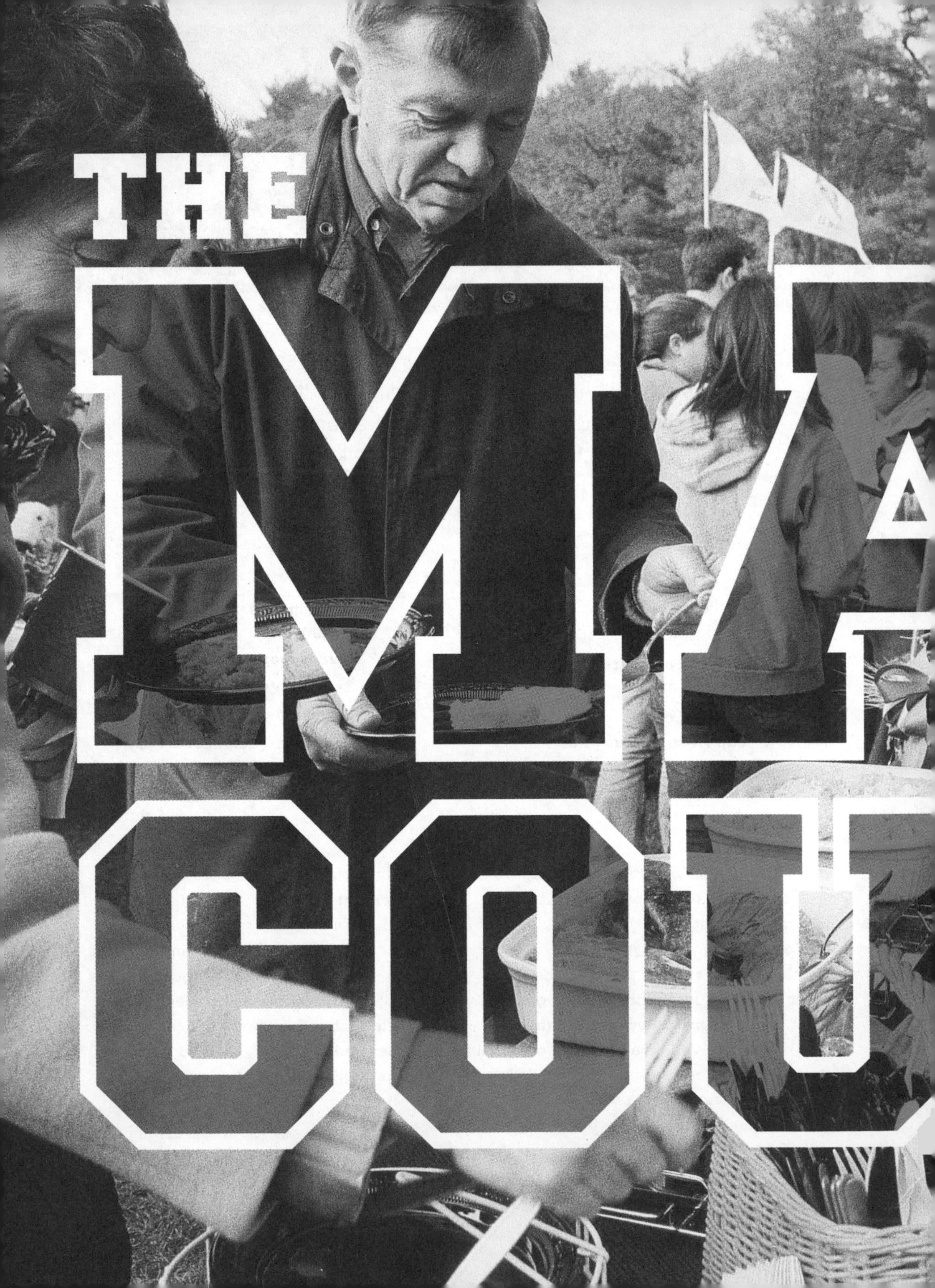

THE M
CO

NN
RSE

The heart and soul of a tailgate party is the main course. It's what separates the pros from those who tailgate with their backseat stacked with pizzas and subs from a local pizzeria. It's the dish you'll be remembered for. In some cases, it will be the most complicated dish you make; it might also be the easiest. If that's the case, don't let on. Accept the accolades graciously. Just be aware that your guests may try to show their appreciation by dumping a cooler of Gatorade over your head.

Fresh from the Grill

Not every tailgate meal has to be cooked on the grill. But you can't call yourself a real tailgater until you've proven your quarterbacking skills by taking snaps standing over the hot coals.

Grill Tips

How hot is hot? You need to know how hot your grill is. Gas grills come with a thermometer. Charcoal grills come with your hand. You'll know how hot your grill is by seeing how long you can hold your open palm 2 to 3 inches over the grill.

1 SECOND = VERY HOT
2 SECONDS = HOT
3 SECONDS = MEDIUM-HOT
4 SECONDS = MEDIUM

These recipes all call for a fire with one of these degrees of heat. If the fire's too hot, the outside of the food will get done way before the inside. If it's not hot enough, you won't get the benefit of the distinctive charred flavor from the grill.

Know where the hot spots are. Each fire is different. No matter how evenly you spread the coals, there will be hotter places on the grill. Rotate your meats so that the pieces on the cooler areas get a turn on higher heat, and vice versa.

Be patient but attentive. Don't turn the meat until it has browned on the bottom to the degree you want.

Employ a two-minute warning. It's much easier to get the meat off the grill at the proper time if you are keeping track of it. Don't start grilling the burgers or brats and then walk away. Give yourself something like a two-minute warning so you can anticipate when the food needs to come off the heat. Don't worry if you sometimes have to cut into one piece of shish kabob or pierce a chicken thigh to see how close it is to being done. This isn't *Iron Chef*.

Know where your receivers are. Make sure you've set aside a place to put the meat once it's done. You've worked so hard to cook the steak properly, you don't want to abandon it while you scrounge for a platter. Have your serving items ready beforehand. And if you plan to slice the meat for your guests, make sure the cutting board is in place and cleared off.

Cooking Chart

These are temperatures at which meat is cooked to the specified doneness. USDA cooking temperature recommendations are somewhat higher.

Beef

Medium-rare = 130° to 135°F
Medium = 135° to 140°F

Pork

Medium-well = 145° to 150°F
(meat will be slightly pink but trichinosis will be killed)

Chicken

Chicken breast = 160°F
Chicken thigh = 165°F

Lamb

Medium-rare = 135° to 140°F
Medium = 140° to 145°F

Beef and Lamb

Every weekend, in football stadiums and NASCAR tracks all over the country, come kickoff time or the call to "start your engines," a whole lot of beef is being digested in the grandstands. Steaks and burgers still reign supreme in these venues. Diet fads and nutritional warnings don't just take a backseat, but are left behind in the garage to make room for another ice chest filled with meat.

Cooking a steak makes the average Joe feel like Mario Batali. He knows that if he buys a big enough piece of meat, gets the grill good and hot, and somehow manages to pull the steak off right when it's done, even Mario, with all his expertise, couldn't do a better job.

And we musn't discount the existential aspects of steak consumption. A man feels more of a man when he's eating a steak. Never mind that he weighs the same as the starting right tackle, only he's 10 inches shorter. Or that his high school football career was tragically cut short due to his lack of size, speed, skill, and ability. When he's eating his steak in the parking lot, in his mind he's down on the field, right there in the huddle, getting his number called for the next play.

And while a nice cut of lamb may not have the same cachet as a steak, it has no shortage of flavor. The recipes here take full advantage of that, knowing that a man can still exude just as much manliness with a double-cut lamb chop in his hand.

GRILLED PORTERHOUSE STEAK

Serves 4

For many serious tailgaters, this steak is what they think of all week, when they're not busy checking their fantasy team stats. It calls for a slightly thicker cut than what you might find on the supermarket shelf. If you can't find steaks this thick, make sure you shorten the cooking time slightly, and get an extra steak. My brother-in-law David of Deluxe Movie Catering turned me on to this foolproof grilling method with two levels of heat.

2 porterhouse steaks (about 3½ pounds total), cut 1½ inches thick
Salt and ground black pepper

At the tailgate Prepare coals for a hot fire. When the coals are ready, arrange them so that one side of the grill is very hot and the other side is medium-hot.

Season both sides of the steaks liberally with salt and pepper. Grill the steaks on the hot side of the grill until nicely browned, 2 to 3 minutes. Turn and grill for 2 to 3 minutes more. Shift the steaks to the medium side and grill for 6 to 7 minutes more for medium-rare, turning once.

Let the steaks rest for 5 minutes before slicing. To serve, slice along the bone to cut away the strip side and filet side. Cut each piece into ¾-inch slices and distribute fairly. Discreetly save the bone to gnaw on later—this is the reward for doing the grilling.

Note Remember to use only tongs to turn the steaks. Never use a fork (even if the guy pictured on your "Kiss the Chef" apron is using one), as it will allow the juices to run freely.

FLANK STEAK WITH CHIPOTLE SAUCE

Serves 4

Once, when my friend Mark Gladstone and I tailgated out at Giants Stadium, we wanted to grill some steak. Since Mark's a teacher, we were on a budget. So I suggested this flank steak, which we served with the incredibly flavorful chipotle sauce. This recipe is supposed to serve 4, but I confess that Mark and I finished it off by ourselves.

CHIPOTLE SAUCE

- **1 tablespoon vegetable oil**
- **1 medium onion, thinly sliced**
- **1 poblano chile, stemmed, seeded, and coarsely chopped**
- **4 scallions, green parts only, chopped**
- **3 tablespoons finely chopped garlic**
- **2 canned chipotle chiles in adobo sauce, coarsely chopped**
- **1 tablespoon chili powder**
- **1 teaspoon ground cumin**
- **½ teaspoon salt**
- **¼ cup water, plus more as needed**

- **1 flank steak (about 1¼ pounds)**
- **2 tablespoons olive oil**
- **Salt and ground black pepper**

At home **For the chipotle sauce:** Place a medium sauté pan over medium-high heat, add the vegetable oil and the onion, poblano chile, and scallions and cook, stirring frequently, until the onion softens, about 8 minutes. Add the garlic, chipotle chiles, chili powder, cumin, and salt and cook for 2 minutes more. Add the ¼ cup water and cook until the liquid is reduced by half, about 2 minutes.

Transfer the mixture to a blender and purée. Add more water, 1 tablespoon at a time, if necessary. The sauce should be the consistency of ketchup. Transfer to a sealable container and refrigerate until you are ready to pack, up to 48 hours.

At the tailgate Prepare coals for a hot fire. Rub the steak with the olive oil and season well with salt and pepper. When the coals are ready, grill the steak for 9 to 10 minutes, turning once, for medium-rare.

Let the steak rest for 5 minutes before cutting it lengthwise into ½-inch slices. Serve topped with a generous helping of the chipotle sauce.

★ ★ ★

CHILI-RUBBED RIB EYES

Serves 4

A lot of folks like grilled rib-eye steaks unadorned. As do I. But this extra bit of seasoning puts them over the top. It's kind of like end-zone celebrations. Some fans see them as foolish posturing. Others think they're "da shizzle." Personally, I think there's room for both perspectives.

4 rib-eye steaks (about 12 ounces each)
¼ cup olive oil
1 tablespoon chili powder
1 tablespoon dried oregano
1 teaspoon garlic powder
1 teaspoon paprika
1 teaspoon ground cumin
1 teaspoon salt
1 teaspoon ground black pepper

At the tailgate Prepare coals for a hot fire.

While the coals are heating, trim away any excess fat from the edge of the steaks. Brush both sides of the steaks with the olive oil.

In a small bowl, combine the chili powder, oregano, garlic powder, paprika, cumin, salt, and pepper. Rub the spice mixture onto both sides of each steak.

When the coals are ready, grill the steaks for 9 minutes, turning once, for medium-rare, 10 to 11 minutes for medium. Serve immediately.

★★★

RED WINE RIB EYES WITH MIXED PEPPER SALSA

Serves 4

The driver is the most prominent member of a race team. He's the one being stopped every two feet behind the pit row after happy hour with requests to sign photos and programs and the back of grandma's shirt. But every NASCAR fan knows that the driver cannot win without a solid team. This includes the car chief, the crew chief, the pit crew, the spotter, the engine specialist, the tire specialist, and, often, the driver's mom—to make sure he gets some sleep before the race. And for all the days they are at the track fine-tuning the car, these people have to be fed. This is the responsibility of the crew chef. The year 2004 saw the creation of the inaugural Crew Chef Challenge. It was won by James Lupo with his red wine and rib-eye recipe, adapted here for everyone to enjoy.

4 rib-eye steaks (about 3 pounds total)
1 cup dry red wine
2 tablespoons Worcestershire sauce
1 medium onion, thinly sliced
4 cloves garlic, coarsely chopped
⅓ cup extra-virgin olive oil
1 teaspoon red pepper flakes
½ teaspoon salt

MIXED PEPPER SALSA

2 tablespoons extra-virgin olive oil
½ teaspoon salt
1 red bell pepper, cored, seeded, and cut lengthwise into 1-inch strips
1 yellow bell pepper, cored, seeded, and cut lengthwise into 1-inch strips
1 green bell pepper, cored, seeded, and cut lengthwise into 1-inch strips
1 medium red onion, cut in half lengthwise and thinly sliced
4 cloves garlic, finely chopped
1 teaspoon fresh thyme, or ½ teaspoon dried thyme
Salt and ground black pepper

At home Place the steaks in a sealable container. Add the wine, Worcestershire sauce, onion, garlic, olive oil, red pepper flakes, and salt. Refrigerate for 12 hours and up to 24 hours.

For the mixed pepper salsa: Place a large skillet over medium-high heat, and let it get hot, about 2 minutes. Add the olive oil; red, yellow, and green bell peppers; and onion and cook until the peppers soften, about 10 minutes. Add the garlic and thyme, season with salt and pepper, and cook for 1 minute more.

Transfer to a sealable bowl and let cool. Refrigerate for up to 2 days.

At the tailgate Prepare coals for a hot fire.

While the coals are ready, remove the steaks from the marinade and pat them dry. Transfer the pepper salsa to a small saucepan.

When the coals are ready, grill the steaks for 9 minutes, turning once, for medium-rare, 10 to 11 minutes for medium. During the last 5 minutes, place the saucepan with the pepper salsa on the grill to reheat.

When the steaks are done, remove them immediately from the grill and serve topped with the pepper salsa.

★ ★ ★

SPICY SKIRT STEAK

Serves 4

Skirt steak is great on the grill. You can do just about anything to it, and it will not fail you. This preparation sparkles with the addition of the roasted lime juice.

- **¼ cup olive oil**
- **¼ cup fresh lime juice (from about 2 large limes)**
- **4 cloves garlic, finely chopped**
- **1 tablespoon ground cumin**
- **1 tablespoon ground coriander**
- **2 skirt steaks (about 3 pounds total), cut in half**
- **1 medium red onion, thinly sliced**
- **1 red bell pepper, cored, seeded, and thinly sliced**
- **¼ cup chopped fresh cilantro**
- **3 limes, cut in half**
- **2 tablespoons hot taco sauce**
- **1 teaspoon salt**

At home One hour before cooking, mix together the olive oil, lime juice, garlic, cumin, and coriander. Place the steaks in a resealable freezer bag and pour in the marinade, making sure the steaks are completely coated.

At the tailgate Prepare coals for a hot fire. When the coals are ready, transfer the skirt steaks directly from the marinade to the grill and cook for 8 to 9 minutes, turning once, for medium-rare, 9 to 10 minutes for medium.

Transfer the steaks to a cutting board and let them rest for 5 minutes. While the steaks are resting, transfer the onion, bell pepper, and cilantro to a medium serving bowl. Place the limes, cut side down, on the grill until they brown slightly, about 4 minutes. Set aside.

Cut the steaks into ½-inch strips, then add them to the bowl with the onion mixture. Season with the hot sauce and salt, then squeeze the grilled limes over everything. Toss together and serve.

FILET MIGNON SANDWICHES

Serves 4

There's something decadent and satisfying about taking this normally precious cut of meat and throwing it between two pieces of white bread with just steak sauce as a garnish. It's very much in keeping with the tailgate spirit and its working-class roots. Still, filet is a bit pricey, so be sure to allow your righteous proletarian anger to get the best of you while it is on the grill.

4 pieces beef tenderloin (about 2 pounds total), cut 1¾ to 2 inches thick
Salt and ground black pepper
8 slices white bread
Steak sauce for serving

At the tailgate Prepare coals for a medium-hot fire. When the coals are ready, assemble them so there is a hot fire on one side and a medium fire on the other.

Season both sides of the meat well with salt and pepper. Cook on the hot side of the grill until nicely browned, 2 to 3 minutes. Turn and grill for 2 to 3 minutes more.

Move the filets to the medium side of the grill and cook for 6 minutes more, turning once, for medium-rare.

Serve on white bread with steak sauce, making sure your guests know this is filet mignon they are eating.

MEATBALL GRINDERS

Serves 8

Growing up in New England, we called these sub sandwiches "grinders." Since there was no place to tailgate outside Fenway, when I was a kid my friends and I would go to one of the great grinder emporiums in Kenmore Square before the game, sneak the sandwiches into the bleachers, and down them with a bottle of Moxie during batting practice. I was eating my grinder and wearing my PF Flyers when I saw Mickey Mantle, then in his last year in the majors, step up to the plate for his turn at batting practice and promptly hit four straight homers—two into the net above the Green Monster, two completely out of the park. Then the Mick walked slowly back to his seat on the Yankee bench. The entire stadium, including the Sox dugout, gave him a standing O. He tipped his cap.

- **2 slices whole wheat bread, cut into ½-inch cubes**
- **¼ cup milk**
- **2 pounds ground sirloin**
- **1 medium onion, grated**
- **½ cup grated Parmesan cheese**
- **1 teaspoon dried oregano**
- **1 teaspoon dried basil**
- **1 teaspoon salt**
- **1 egg, lightly beaten**
- **¼ cup olive oil**
- **1 jar (32 ounces) spaghetti sauce**
- **4 soft Italian sub breads or 8 rolls about 8 by 5 inches**
- **4 ounces provolone cheese, thinly sliced**

At home Preheat the oven to 375°F.

Put the bread cubes in a large bowl, add the milk, and let the bread soak for a few minutes to soften.

Add the ground sirloin to the bread, along with the onion, Parmesan, oregano, basil, salt, and egg and mix together with your hands until well combined. Shape into sixteen 1½-inch balls.

Place a large skillet over medium-high heat and let it get hot, about 2 minutes. Add the olive oil and spread it evenly over the pan. Add half the meatballs and brown them entirely, 6 to 8 minutes, turning them every minute or so. Transfer to an 11-by-17-inch casserole. Repeat to cook the remaining meatballs.

Pour the spaghetti sauce over the meatballs and bake, covered, for 12 minutes. Remove the cover and bake for 6 minutes more. Remove the pan from the oven and let the meatballs cool. Transfer to a sealable container and refrigerate until you are ready to pack, up to 24 hours.

At the tailgate If using Italian sub breads, cut them in half crosswise. Slice the sub bread halves or the rolls open lengthwise, but not cutting all the way through; leave one side attached like a hinge. Fill each one with 4 meatballs and top with some slices of provolone. Top with some of the sauce. Wrap each grinder in aluminum foil. Heat them over a medium fire for 6 minutes, turning once.

Note If you aren't bringing a grill, cook or reheat the meatballs so they come out of the oven just before leaving for the tailgate. Then assemble the grinders at home, wrap them in a double layer of aluminum foil, and serve them warm at the tailgate.

BARBECUED SHORT RIBS

Serves 6

Packers fans have their brats. Saints fans have their gumbo. The Houston Texans fans love their brisket. But someone needs to adopt these short ribs. They are worthy of being elevated to that kind of status. I imagine a parking lot packed with delirious fans, each holding a hefty short rib bone in his or her hand, smiling with rapture and delight. Surely there's a team out there looking for such an arrangement.

- **2 tablespoons olive oil**
- **6 large short ribs (5 to 6 pounds total)**
- **1 large onion, coarsely chopped**
- **6 cloves garlic, finely chopped**
- **½ cup ketchup**
- **¼ cup fresh orange juice**
- **2 tablespoons fresh lemon juice**
- **2 tablespoons brown sugar**
- **2 tablespoons molasses**
- **2 tablespoons Worcestershire sauce**
- **1 tablespoon chili powder**
- **1 teaspoon red pepper flakes**
- **1 teaspoon ground cumin**
- **1 teaspoon Dijon mustard**
- **1 cup Homemade Barbecue Sauce (page 168)**

At home Heat the olive oil over medium-high heat in a large pot, preferably a Dutch oven, and brown the short ribs well on all sides, about 20 minutes.

Remove the ribs and pour out the excess fat from the pan. Add the onion and cook until it softens slightly, about 5 minutes. Add the garlic and cook for 2 minutes more. Add the ketchup, orange juice, lemon juice, brown sugar, molasses, Worcestershire sauce, chili powder, red pepper flakes, cumin, and mustard and bring the mixture to a boil. Return the ribs to the pot, reduce the heat to low, and simmer until the meat is soft and almost falling from the bone, about 1 hour and 15 minutes.

Remove the pot from the heat and let cool. Transfer the ribs to a sealable container.

At the tailgate Prepare coals for a medium fire. When the coals are ready, arrange the ribs on the grill and cook for 12 minutes, turning and basting with the barbecue sauce several times.

Serve immediately.

★ ★ ★

GRILLED LEG OF LAMB JAMAICAN STYLE

Serves 6

One fall afternoon, my sons and I decided to tailgate out at Randalls Island. This is a unique tailgating experience. Randalls is one of two islands off Manhattan (Wards Island is the other) devoted to ball fields of all kinds. I cooked this lamb at one of the grills the city provides there, and we ate on an adjacent picnic table overlooking the East River. We then wandered around the more than two dozen fields, watching intensely played games of soccer, baseball, cricket, flag football, and the tail end of a rugby match. Only in New York.

MANGO RELISH

- 2 tablespoons olive oil
- 1 medium onion, finely chopped
- 1 red bell pepper, cored, seeded, and finely chopped
- 1 scallion, green part only, finely chopped
- 1-inch piece of fresh ginger, peeled, and finely chopped
- 4 cloves garlic, finely chopped
- 1 jalapeño chile, stemmed, seeded, and finely chopped
- 2 mangoes, peeled, pitted, and chopped
- ¼ cup fresh lime juice (from about 2 large limes)
- 1 teaspoon salt

MARINADE

- 2 tablespoons olive oil
- 1 large onion, finely chopped
- 1 scallion, green part only, finely chopped
- 6 cloves garlic, finely chopped
- 1 jalapeño chile, stemmed, seeded, and finely chopped
- 1 teaspoon ground allspice
- 2 tablespoons fresh lime juice
- ¼ cup dark rum

- 1 boneless leg of lamb (4 to 5 pounds), butterflied

At home **For the mango relish:** Place a medium sauté pan over medium heat, add the olive oil and the onion, bell pepper, scallion, ginger, garlic, and jalapeño and cook until the vegetables begin to soften, about 4 minutes.

Add the mangoes, lime juice, and salt and stir until combined. Transfer to a bowl and let cool. Transfer to a sealable container and refrigerate until you are ready to pack, up to 24 hours.

For the marinade: Place the olive oil, onion, scallion, garlic, jalapeño, allspice, lime juice, and rum in a blender and purée until just smooth.

Coat both sides of the lamb with the marinade, place it in a sealable container, and refrigerate for at least 4 hours and up to 24 hours.

At the tailgate Prepare coals for a medium-hot fire. When the coals are ready, grill the lamb for 22 minutes, turning once.

With a sharp knife, cut away the thinner middle section of the leg and transfer it to a platter. Leave the thicker end pieces to cook 5 to 7 minutes longer, turning once.

Let the lamb rest for 5 minutes before cutting it on the diagonal into thin slices. If some sections are still too rare, lay the slices on the grill for a few seconds on each side.

Serve with the mango relish.

★ ★ ★

GRILLED LAMB CHOPS

Serves 4

Standing around the grill in the parking lot, among a throng of like-minded fans, with everyone getting geared up for the game, is the perfect place to dispense with your manners. So grab a lamb chop by the bone and eat it with relish and gusto.

¼ cup olive oil
¼ cup chopped fresh parsley
¼ cup chopped fresh mint
¼ cup chopped fresh basil, or 2 tablespoons dried basil
6 cloves garlic, finely chopped
1 tablespoon salt
1 tablespoon ground black pepper
½ teaspoon ground cumin
8 rib lamb chops

At home Measure the olive oil, parsley, mint, basil, garlic, salt, pepper, and cumin into a sealable container and refrigerate until ready to pack, up to 4 hours.

At the tailgate Prepare coals for a hot fire. While the coals are heating, pour the olive oil mixture into a wide bowl or pie plate and set it near the grill.

When the coals are ready, working with 2 chops at a time, dip them in the olive oil mixture before placing them on the grill. Work quickly to get all the chops on the grill as close to the same time as possible.

Grill the chops for 5 to 6 minutes, turning once, for medium-rare, 6 to 7 minutes for medium. Serve immediately.

Pork

You can't think of pork without thinking of ribs. And before a big race or game, many parking lots in the Mid-Atlantic and Deep South are a sea of smoked ribs. Barbecue aficionados can close their eyes and tell by the aroma of the sauce what region they are in. But pork comes in many shapes and sizes, and tailgaters in all areas of the country are discovering them. Some people shy away from cooking pork because you can't put ketchup on it. They worry that it requires some kind of sauce, which means serving pork is twice as much work as, say, grilling a steak. While this is mostly true, the payoff for making the marinade or sauce is well worth the extra effort. Cooking pork also requires more finesse on the grill—more Tiki Barber than Jerome Bettis. You'll need to be attentive to your grill's temperature, especially when dealing with leaner cuts of pork, which can dry out quickly.

TAILGATING TALES

OAXACA ON THE HUDSON

Some of the best tailgating food I've had was during the championship game of New York City's Mexican Soccer League. The field is shoe-horned into a long, narrow strip of packed dirt along the Hudson River in the upper reaches of Manhattan. It's not unusual for an errant shot to wind up in the water. There are no bleachers. There is no parking lot. (Parking is, in fact, about a half-mile away on Dyckeman Street, which, fortunately, is in an area of Manhattan where, at the moment of this writing, you do not have to feed the parking meters.) Several women set up an improvised cooking area, with oil drum grills and gas cookers and coolers filled with bright orange soda. A pot of *mofungo* simmered continuously. There was a taco press and a *comal* for cooking them. Salsas were in well-seasoned plastic containers that bore the tint of their contents. The food was outrageous, the soccer just as exciting.

★ ★ ★

GRILLED PORK TACOS

Makes 8 tacos

These tacos are essential Mexican cooking—fresh, earthy flavors of chiles and meat heightened with cilantro and lime. No yellow cheese. No packets of too-sweet taco sauce.

6 dried ancho chiles, stemmed, seeded, and torn into large pieces
2 cups very hot water
1 medium onion, cut into quarters, plus 1 cup finely chopped onion
4 cloves garlic, coarsely chopped
1 teaspoon dried oregano
1 teaspoon salt, plus more for seasoning
½ teaspoon ground black pepper, plus more for seasoning
1 teaspoon ground cumin
¼ teaspoon ground cloves
2 pork tenderloins (about 2 pounds total)
1 cup coarsely chopped fresh cilantro
8 corn tortillas
2 limes, cut in half
Hot sauce for serving

At home Soak the ancho chiles in the hot water until they soften, about 1 hour. You may need to weigh the chiles down with a small plate so they will be fully submerged.

Transfer the chiles and 1 cup of the soaking liquid to a blender along with the quartered onion, garlic, oregano, 1 teaspoon salt, ½ teaspoon pepper, cumin, and cloves and purée until smooth. Transfer the mixture to a bowl.

Season the pork tenderloins with salt and pepper and then cover them with half of the chile purée, reserving the other half for later. Transfer the coated pork tenderloins to a sealable container and refrigerate until you are ready to pack, at least 1 hour or up to 6 hours.

In a small, sealable container, mix together the chopped onion and cilantro and refrigerate until ready to pack.

At the tailgate Prepare coals for a medium-hot fire. While the coals are heating, combine the cilantro and chopped onion in a small serving bowl and set aside. When the coals are ready, grill the tenderloins until they are almost entirely cooked through, with just the smallest hint of pink in the center, 12 to 14 minutes, turning every few minutes to brown them evenly.

Remove the tenderloins from the grill and let them rest for 5 minutes. While they are resting, cover the grill with tortillas, cooking them until they soften and just start to show some brown spots, about 1 minute per side. Stack the hot tortillas on a plate under a clean kitchen cloth.

Cut the pork into ½-inch slices and transfer to a bowl. Add the remaining chile purée and toss the pork slices in it. Squeeze one of the limes over the pork. Squeeze the other one into the onion-cilantro mixture.

To assemble the tacos, have people put some sliced pork and a tablespoon of the onion-cilantro mixture in a tortilla. Top with some hot sauce, fold, and eat.

★ ★ ★

GRILLED PORK TENDERLOINS WITH MAPLE MUSTARD GLAZE

Serves 4

This dish has a sweet-and-sour thing going. The tenderloins are cut from the whole loin and are about 2 inches across and 12 inches long. It's an easy recipe to prepare, but like the great Joe Morris of the New York Giants, it packs a lot of flavor into its small frame.

½ cup salt
½ cup sugar
2 pork tenderloins (about 2 pounds total)
¼ cup pure maple syrup
3 tablespoons Dijon mustard
1 teaspoon cider vinegar
½ teaspoon ground black pepper

At home Dissolve the salt and sugar in a large bowl half full of cold water. Place the pork tenderloins in the bowl and refrigerate for at least 1 hour and up to 4 hours. Remove the pork from the brine and pat dry. Transfer to a resealable freezer bag and refrigerate until ready to pack.

In a small sealable container, combine the maple syrup, mustard, vinegar, and pepper and refrigerate until ready to pack.

At the tailgate Prepare coals for a medium-hot fire. When the coals are ready, grill the tenderloins for 8 minutes, turning every few minutes to brown them evenly. Baste them with half the sauce and cook for 4 to 6 minutes more, turning and basting several times, until they are almost entirely cooked through, with just the smallest hint of pink in the center.

Transfer to a cutting board and let rest for 5 minutes. Slice on the diagonal and serve with the remaining maple-mustard sauce.

Note I've made fabulous sandwiches with this pork, using a crusty baguette, a little lettuce and red onion, and a healthy shmear of maple mustard.

TAILGATING TALES

I LOVE THE SMELL OF PORK STEAK IN THE MORNING

Michael Repovich works in downtown St. Louis. In the summer, when the Cardinals are playing a weekday day game, about an hour before the first pitch, if the wind is right, the aroma of brats and other meats cooking on the grills in the parking lot starts wafting in the direction of his office. Needless to say, not much work gets done until the game starts, as suddenly everyone has become too hungry to concentrate. Besides brats, which are (big surprise) popular in St. Louis, Michael also discovered that he was basking in the aroma of a favorite local dish, the pork steak. Die-hard Cardinal tailgaters are devoted to these large, 1-inch-thick cuts. Michael remembers asking for them in an exclusive butcher shop in Boston when he was working there one summer, but the guy behind the counter looked at him as though he had three heads. Fortunately, he is now back in a more rational universe. You should be able to find pork steaks in the meat section of most large supermarkets.

★ ★ ★

GRILLED HERB-CRUSTED PORK STEAKS

Serves 4

It's not customary to cook pork medium-rare as you would a beef steak, but you still want it to be moist and flavorful. A short brining does the trick. Set up your signed 8-by-10 photos of Cardinal greats Stan Musial and Bob Gibson before serving.

- **½ cup salt**
- **½ cup sugar**
- **4 pork steaks, cut 1 inch thick**
- **¼ cup olive oil**
- **8 cloves garlic, finely chopped**
- **¼ cup chopped fresh parsley**
- **1 tablespoon dried thyme**
- **1 tablespoon dried basil**
- **2 teaspoons onion powder**
- **2 teaspoons salt**
- **1 teaspoon ground black pepper**

At home Dissolve the salt and sugar in a large bowl half full of cold water. Place the pork steaks in the bowl and refrigerate for at least 1 hour and up to 4 hours. Remove the steaks from the brine and pat dry. Brush both sides with the olive oil.

In a small bowl, mix together the garlic, parsley, thyme, basil, onion powder, salt, and pepper. Rub into the steaks and let them sit for 1 hour at room temperature, or transfer to a sealable container and refrigerate for up to 4 hours.

At the tailgate Prepare coals for a medium-hot fire. When the coals are ready, grill the steaks, turning once, until they are cooked through, about 8 minutes. Serve immediately.

BONELESS PORK CHOPS WITH CHILI CITRUS CRUST

Serves 4

These chops have a fabulous taste. It's the perfect balance of spice and sweetness. This is the kind of food I'd drive out to the stadium to tailgate for even if I didn't have a ticket to the game.

- **¼ cup fresh orange juice**
- **¼ cup fresh cilantro leaves**
- **4 cloves garlic**
- **2 tablespoons fresh lime juice**
- **2 tablespoons olive oil**
- **1 tablespoon ground cumin**
- **1 tablespoon chili powder**
- **1 tablespoon sweet paprika**
- **1 tablespoon ground coriander**
- **½ teaspoon cayenne**
- **1 teaspoon salt**
- **4 loin pork chops, cut 1¼ inch thick**
- **1 cup Mango Relish (page 72)**

At home Put the orange juice, cilantro, garlic, lime juice, olive oil, cumin, chili powder, paprika, coriander, cayenne, and salt in a blender and pulse until smooth, about 6 pulses.

Using half the marinade, coat both sides of the chops. Place the chops in a resealable freezer bag and refrigerate until you are ready to pack, up to 4 hours. Transfer the remaining marinade to a sealable container and refrigerate until ready to pack.

At the tailgate Prepare coals for a medium-hot fire. When the coals are ready, arrange them so that the coals are all on one side of the grill.

Cook the chops over the coals until nicely browned, about 2 minutes, then turn and grill for 2 minutes more. Transfer the chops to the cooler side of the grill and baste them with the reserved marinade. Cover the grill, making sure the bottom and top vents are open, and grill, turning once, and basting again, until the chops are just cooked through, about 10 minutes more. I like them when they're still a bit pink in the center, but that's up to you. Serve immediately with the mango relish.

★ ★ ★

GRILLED PEACH-GLAZED HAM STEAKS

Serves 4

Great for a brisk fall afternoon, this is a fast, easy, and versatile recipe. The canned peaches harken back to another era—back when players didn't celebrate after every tackle and there wasn't such a stigma attached to using ingredients that came from a can.

CITRUS-GINGER SAUCE

- 1 lemon
- 1 orange
- 1 grapefruit
- 1 teaspoon extra-virgin olive oil
- 2 teaspoons finely chopped fresh ginger
- 1 teaspoon finely chopped garlic
- 1 teaspoon finely chopped shallot
- ½ cup white wine

PEACH GLAZE

- 1 can (12 ounces) peaches, drained
- 2 tablespoons mustard
- 2 tablespoons brown sugar
- 1 jalapeño chile, stemmed, seeded, and finely chopped

- 2 center-cut ham steaks (about 1 pound each)

At home **For the citrus-ginger sauce:** Zest the lemon entirely, and then mince the zest. Cut the lemon, orange, and grapefruit in half crosswise. Scoop the meat out of the sections of each half of fruit with a serrated grapefruit spoon. Transfer to a bowl and squeeze any remaining juice from the fruit over it. Add the lemon zest.

Mix together the olive oil, ginger, garlic, shallot, and wine in a small saucepan and bring to a boil over medium heat. Reduce the heat to low and simmer until the liquid is reduced by half, about 4 minutes.

Add the fruit and zest and cook for 1 minute more. Let the sauce cool, and then transfer to a sealable container and refrigerate until you are ready to pack, up to 4 hours.

For the peach glaze: Place the peaches, mustard, brown sugar, and jalapeño in a blender or food processor and process until smooth.

Cover each side of the ham steaks with the peach mixture and transfer to a sealable container just large enough to hold them. Refrigerate until you are ready to pack, up to 4 hours.

At the tailgate Prepare coals for a medium-hot fire. When the coals are ready, grill the ham steaks for 10 minutes, turning once. Serve immediately with the sauce.

★ ★ ★

SOUTHWESTERN-STYLE BABY BACK RIBS

Serves 4

I once considered making more authentic smoked ribs for a tailgate party and, in the planning, realized that not only would I need to be at the parking lot hours before everyone else, but my grill was not large enough to smoke enough ribs for everyone in my party. And to try to pass off just "a taste" of barbecued ribs is like trying to arm-tackle Priest Holmes. So it was a choice between shelling out for another grill or devising another method of cooking the ribs. Baking them first in a slow oven produced moist, flavorful meat I then had only to finish on the grill.

1 tablespoon dried thyme
1 tablespoon granulated garlic
1 tablespoon onion powder
1 tablespoon brown sugar
1 tablespoon paprika
1 tablespoon chili powder
1 teaspoon dried rosemary
1 teaspoon salt
1 teaspoon ground black pepper
3 racks baby back ribs (about 5 pounds total)
3 cups Homemade Barbecue Sauce (page 168)

At home In a small bowl, mix together the thyme, garlic, onion powder, brown sugar, paprika, chili powder, rosemary, salt, and pepper. Rub the spice mixture over both sides of the ribs. Wrap in plastic and refrigerate overnight or up to 24 hours.

Preheat the oven to 325°F. Unwrap the ribs and place them on a baking sheet. Cover completely with aluminum foil. Bake for 1 hour and 10 minutes. Remove the foil and let the ribs cool. Refrigerate them, wrapped in plastic, until you are ready to pack, up to 24 hours.

Just before leaving, cut the racks into individual ribs and place them in a large, sealable container. Add 1 cup of the barbecue sauce and stir so all the ribs are coated.

At the tailgate Prepare coals for a medium fire. When the coals are ready, grill the ribs for 10 minutes, until they are lightly charred and heated through, turning them several times and applying several more moppings of sauce.

Serve the ribs hot, accompanied by more sauce.

SMOKED SPARERIBS

Serves 4

The one positive to be found in football games getting longer every season is that there is now sufficient time to smoke a rack of ribs. The frequency of TV time-outs and reviewed plays has allowed the valiant keepers of the tailgating flame, those who remain in the parking lot, sufficient time to prepare the grill and, without rushing, smoke their ribs to the perfect stage of succulence. If you are lucky enough to be connected with one of these men, it means you can be casually enjoying a delicious postgame treat while everyone else fights the traffic leaving the stadium.

1 tablespoon brown sugar
1 tablespoon paprika
1 tablespoon chili powder
2 teaspoons ground cumin
2 teaspoons ground black pepper
2 teaspoons salt
2 racks trimmed spareribs (about 4 pounds total)
2 cups hickory or other hardwood chips
1 cup Homemade Barbecue Sauce (page 168)

At home In a small bowl, mix together the brown sugar, paprika, chili powder, cumin, pepper, and salt. Rub into both sides of the racks of ribs. Let them sit for 2 hours at room temperature, or wrap in plastic and refrigerate for up to 12 hours.

At the tailgate One hour before grilling, soak the wood chips in enough water to cover.

Prepare coals for a medium-hot fire. While the coals are heating, make 2 packages of wood chips. Lay a 12-inch, double layer of aluminum foil on a work surface. Place half the wood chips in the center, then fold to make a neat package. Poke 6 holes in the top to release the smoke during cooking. Repeat with the remaining wood chips.

When the coals are ready, arrange them on one side of the grill in as consolidated a pile as possible. Place one of the packages of wood chips on top of the coals. Arrange the ribs on the side of the rack opposite the coals. Cover the grill and open the top vents.

Grill the ribs for about 3 hours, adding a few more coals every hour. Halfway through cooking, place the second package of wood chips on the coals and turn the racks of ribs.

Transfer the racks to a cutting board and cut them into individual ribs. Serve with the barbecue sauce.

★ ★ ★

CUBAN SANDWICHES

Serves 2

Some aluminum foil and a brick make this classic sandwich possible on your grill. Grill a few sandwiches, mash some mint and make some *mojitos,* and toast some of the great Cuban baseball players–José Méndez, Armando Marsans, Tony Oliva, Zoilo Versalles, Tony Perez, Luis "El Tiante" Tiante, and the irrepressible Orestes "Minnie" Minoso.

2 sub-shaped soft, sweet rolls, about 7 inches long, or a section of French or Italian bread

2 tablespoons mayonnaise

2 tablespoons mustard

4 ounces smoked ham, thinly sliced

4 ounces roast pork, thinly sliced

2 ounces Swiss cheese, sliced

6 thin slices tomato

6 thin slices dill pickle

1 tablespoon butter

1 brick

At the tailgate Slice the rolls and spread the mayonnaise on one side, mustard on the other. Arrange the ham, pork, cheese, tomatoes, and pickle in the roll. Lightly butter the outside of the rolls.

Prepare coals for a medium fire. Wrap the brick in aluminum foil. When the coals are ready, lay a double layer of foil on the grill. Place the sandwiches on the foil. Place the brick over both sandwiches and press down gently. Grill until the bottom of the bread is browned and the cheese starts to melt, 2 to 3 minutes. Turn, replace the brick, and grill for 2 minutes more. Serve hot.

Note More bricks can facilitate cooking more sandwiches at the same time.

TAILGATING TRANSCENDED

There are tailgaters who never miss a game, who have their spot in the parking lot that everyone knows belongs to them. They have their cooking routines down pat and are so familiar with the walk to their seats that they are able to time their arrival to coincide exactly with the coin toss. These are true tailgaters—devoted, consistent, passionate. But yet another breed of tailgater exists—those rare individuals who operate on a higher, more transcendent level. These are the select few who, because of the purity of their devotion to tailgating, never enter the stadium. You can identify them most easily just before game time, when the parking lot is a beehive of activity, with people scrambling to pack up and furtively checking to make sure they didn't forget their tickets on the kitchen counter. They are the mavericks who are making no move to leave. They don't pack up because they have more cooking to do. They don't check for their tickets because they have no tickets. Instead, they adjust the antenna on their radio or portable TV, straighten up a bit, wipe off the cutting board, and get ready for another round of food—the postgame tailgate. We should all offer a toast to these men who have reached a higher state of tailgate enlightenment.

Chicken and Gator

While chicken will never replace steak among the hard-core, beer-guzzling, face-painted tailgating crowd, it has a secure spot on the serving table among family tailgaters all across America. A grill packed with chicken doesn't have the visceral sensation of one crammed with 2-inch-thick steaks, but chicken can be versatile. It adapts to a variety of flavors and culinary situations. It's like a linebacker who can both rush the passer and cover a wide-out running a deep post. In general, grilling chicken requires a bit more attention than steaks, so refrain from too many tailgating toasts until after the chicken comes off the grill. As for alligator, just don't cook a live one.

★ ★ ★

TERIYAKI CHICKEN CUTLETS

Serves 6

Late October can be a busy time. Baseball's postseason is in full swing (literally), college football is heating up, the NBA preseason has started, and enough NFL games have been played to determine which teams were overrated in the off-season and which might be this year's Cinderella story. With so much going on, you sometimes need a simple, flavorful, and easy-to-prepare main course that you know everyone is going to like. This is it.

¼ cup soy sauce
2 tablespoons brown sugar
1 tablespoon dark (Asian) sesame oil
1 teaspoon curry powder
1 teaspoon ground ginger
6 boneless, skinless chicken breasts

At home In a small container, mix together the soy sauce, brown sugar, sesame oil, curry powder, and ginger. Refrigerate until you are ready to pack, up to 1 day.

Place the chicken breasts in a resealable freezer bag along with the soy mixture, making sure they are coated on all sides. Refrigerate until you are ready to pack, up to 4 hours.

At the tailgate Prepare coals for a medium fire. When the coals are ready, arrange the chicken breasts on the grill without touching, reserving the marinade. Grill until they are nicely browned, 3 to 4 minutes. Brush with the marinade, turn, and grill until they are cooked through, 3 to 4 minutes more. Serve immediately.

★ ★ ★

BARBECUED CHICKEN SANDWICHES

Serves 4

Making this dish is kind of like taking a knee at the end of the game to run out the clock. Not a lot of effort, but you're certain of coming away with a victory.

4 boneless, skinless chicken breasts, pounded flat
2 tablespoons olive oil
2 tablespoons Cajun seasoning
1 cup Homemade Barbecue Sauce (page 168)
4 soft rolls, sliced in half
Lettuce and sliced red onion for serving

At the tailgate Prepare coals for a medium fire.

While the coals are heating, brush the chicken breasts with the olive oil, then rub them with the Cajun seasoning.

When the coals are ready, grill the chicken breasts until they are nicely browned, about 3 minutes. Turn and grill for 2 minutes more. Mop the breasts liberally with the barbecue sauce, turn, and grill for another 2 minutes, mopping with sauce and turning one more time.

Transfer the chicken breasts to a platter. Serve with the rolls, lettuce, onion, and lots more barbecue sauce.

CHAMPIONS

★ ★ ★

GRILLED CHICKEN THIGHS IN ADOBO SAUCE

Serves 4

I can say without equivocation you have never had better chicken thighs.

6 **dried ancho chiles, stemmed, seeded, and torn into large pieces**
2 **cups very hot water**
4 **cloves garlic, coarsely chopped**
2 **teaspoons sugar**
1 **teaspoon dried oregano**
1½ **teaspoons salt**
½ **teaspoon ground black pepper**
½ **teaspoon ground cumin**
¼ **teaspoon ground cloves**
8 **chicken thighs (about 2½ pounds total), skins removed**
2 **tablespoons olive oil**
1 **cup chicken broth**
2 **tablespoons fresh lime juice**
Chopped scallions for garnish

At home Soak the ancho chiles in the hot water until they soften, about 1 hour. You may need to weigh the chiles down with a small plate so they will be fully submerged.

Transfer the chiles and the soaking liquid to a blender, along with the garlic, 1 teaspoon of the sugar, the oregano, 1 teaspoon of the salt, the pepper, cumin, and cloves. Purée until smooth.

Place the chicken thighs in a resealable freezer bag and add half the chile mixture. Make sure the thighs are completely coated. Refrigerate until you are ready to pack, up to 6 hours.

While the thighs are marinating, place a skillet, preferably cast iron, over high heat, and let it get very hot, about 2 minutes. Add the olive oil and spread it evenly over the pan. Add the remaining chile mixture and cook, stirring continuously, until it thickens, about 5 minutes. Add the chicken broth and stir to combine. When the mixture comes to a boil, reduce the heat to low and simmer the sauce until it is thickened and reduced by half, about 18 minutes. Season the sauce with the remaining teaspoon of sugar, the lime juice, and the remaining ½ teaspoon salt, and remove from the heat. Let cool and transfer to a sealable container. Refrigerate until you are ready to pack.

At the tailgate Prepare coals for a medium-hot fire. When the coals are ready, transfer the chicken to the grill directly from the marinade and grill the chicken thighs until they are nicely browned, about 6 minutes. Turn and grill for 6 minutes more. Baste with the marinade and cook for about 8 minutes more, turning and basting every 2 minutes, until the juices run clear and the meat is no longer pink near the bone.

Serve topped with the chile sauce, and garnish with chopped scallions.

GATOR STEAKS

Serves 4

Those who eat gator are proud of it. You can find gator in chilis and fillet of gator tenderloin on grills in parking lots around the South, especially at tailgate parties before Florida games, home of the Gators. This is the simplest way of cooking gator, and it allows you to appreciate its distinctive flavor, which falls somewhere between pork and chicken. Soaking the steaks in milk for a few hours helps tenderize the meat. Serve the teeth on the side.

4 gator tail steaks (about 3 pounds total)
4 cups milk
1 teaspoon cayenne
1 tablespoon dried rosemary
2 tablespoons olive oil
Salt and ground black pepper

At home Soak the steaks in a bowl with the milk, cayenne, and rosemary. Refrigerate for 2 to 4 hours. Remove the steaks from the marinade and pat dry. Transfer to a sealable container or freezer bag and refrigerate until you are ready to pack.

At the tailgate Prepare coals for a medium-hot fire. When the coals are ready, brush the steaks on both sides with the olive oil and season with salt and pepper.

Grill the steaks until they are just cooked through, 8 to 9 minutes, turning once. Despite its rough exterior, gator has a rather delicate flavor, so be sure not to overcook the steaks.

Serve immediately.

K
VEHICLES PARKED
OUTSIDE OF
MARKED STALLS
WILL BE TOWED.
SEC.32.4.2. S.F.
TRAFFIC CODE

Fish and Vegetables

A main course of fish is not what one one usually associates with a serious tailgate party. But sometimes it's a welcome change of pace, especially when it's prepared on the grill. Old-school tailgaters need to acknowledge that the tailgate world is changing. It is no longer solely the domain of the meat eater. Eventually you'll find yourself tailgating with someone (most likely a woman) who might want some fish or grilled vegetables and you'll be glad you're prepared.

★ ★ ★

GRILLED VEGETABLE SANDWICHES WITH GOAT CHEESE

Serves 4

Every once in a while you come across a vegetarian in your tailgating crowd. Rather than relegate him or her to a meal of cotton candy and pretzels from one of the hawkers at the stadium, you can throw this sandwich together without too much fuss.

- **4 slices eggplant, cut ¾ inch thick**
- **1 large onion, cut into ½-inch slices**
- **1 red bell pepper, cored, seeded, and quartered lengthwise**
- **2 large portobello mushrooms, dark gill scraped away, cut into ¾-inch slices**
- **¾ cup Italian dressing**
- **8 ounces goat cheese, sliced**
- **1 ciabatta bread or 4 French rolls**

At the tailgate Prepare coals for a medium fire. While the coals are heating, liberally brush the eggplant, onion, bell pepper, and mushrooms with ½ cup of the dressing.

When the coals are ready, grill the eggplant and mushroom slices until they are lightly browned, about 4 minutes. Turn and grill for about 4 minutes more.

Grill the onion and bell pepper until they are lightly browned, 4 to 5 minutes. Turn and grill for 4 to 5 minutes more. Scrape off any charred bits of skin from the bell pepper.

To assemble the sandwiches, cut the ciabatta crosswise into 4 equal pieces, and then slice open and layer the vegetables on the bottom halves. Top with a few slices of the goat cheese. Spread a tablespoon of the dressing inside each top half. Serve warm.

Note The vegetables can all be grilled, broiled, or cooked in a skillet at home. Wrap each sandwich in aluminum foil and reheat on the grill at the tailgate before serving.

RED SNAPPER WITH POTATOES AND SPINACH IN FOIL

Serves 4

In France, this kind of cooking is called *en papillote.* For tailgating purposes, it's called *en foil.* It's a whole meal in each packet. You need only slide it off the foil and onto a plate to seem like a genius. You can have this dish on hand for anyone (the women) who wants to eat a lighter meal (though having 2 brats instead of 3 seems to me to be a perfectly viable "lighter" option). And since the fish is entirely wrapped in foil, the steaks and burgers don't even have to look at it while they are sizzling blissfully on the grill.

2 tablespoons olive oil
12 ounces red or waxy potatoes, sliced as thinly as possible
Salt and ground black pepper
4 cups spinach leaves (about 4 ounces), washed
4 red snapper fillets
2 tomatoes, thinly sliced
12 basil leaves

At home Cut four 16-inch pieces of aluminum foil and lay them on a work surface. Brush the center of each piece of foil with some of the olive oil.

Arrange 4 or 5 potato slices in the center of each piece of foil in a single layer. Season lightly with salt and pepper. Place a bed of spinach over the potatoes. Lay a snapper fillet skin side down over the spinach, and season lightly with salt and pepper.

Lay 2 or 3 tomato slices on the fish and arrange 3 basil leaves over them. Drizzle with the remaining olive oil.

Bring the long ends of the foil together and fold them tightly several times. Then fold up the sides to make a neat, sealed packet. Place the packets in a sealable container and refrigerate until you are ready to pack, up to 6 hours.

At the tailgate Prepare coals for a medium fire. When the coals are ready, place the fish packets on the grill and cook for 14 minutes.

Open the packets carefully to avoid the escaping steam, and serve.

★ ★ ★

SMOKED SIDE OF SALMON

Serves 6

You may not want to get to the stadium early enough to smoke a brisket, but you should have enough time to smoke a side of salmon. Hot off the grill, it's a flavor as rich and wondrous as anything you've had. Make sure you have a long platter ready to receive it once it's smoked. Use two long spatulas to remove the side of salmon from the grill and keep it somewhat intact for the presentation. Then get out of the way, because it won't be intact for long.

1 cup sugar

1 cup kosher salt

4 cups water

1 whole side of salmon (1½ to 2 pounds), pinbones removed

2 cups hickory or other hardwood chips

2 tablespoons olive oil

3 tablespoons Cajun seasoning

At home In a large mixing bowl, dissolve the sugar and salt in the water. Add a tray of ice cubes, then place the salmon in the bowl and make sure it is completely submerged in the mixture. Brine the salmon in the refrigerator for 3 hours. While the salmon is brining, soak the wood chips in water to cover.

After 3 hours, remove the salmon from the brine and pat it dry. Rub both sides with the olive oil, and rub the flesh side with the Cajun seasoning. Place on a platter and wrap well with plastic. Refrigerate until you are ready to pack, up to 2 hours.

At the tailgate Prepare coals for a medium fire, making sure the bottom vents are fully open.

While the coals are heating, make 2 packages of wood chips. Lay a 12-inch, double layer of aluminum foil on a work surface. Place half the wood chips in the center, then fold to make a neat package. Poke 6 holes in the top to release the smoke during cooking. Repeat with the remaining wood chips.

When the coals are ready, place a package of wood chips on the coals and set the rack in position. Bring the platter with the salmon to the grill and slide the salmon onto the rack, skin side down, on the side of the rack directly opposite the coals. Cover the grill and open the top vents.

Grill the salmon for 1 hour and 10 minutes, adding the second package of wood chips about halfway through, or when the first one stops smoking.

Remove with a pair of spatulas, ideally with someone holding the cleaned platter nearby, ready to receive the salmon.

★ ★ ★

WASABI-GLAZED GRILLED SALMON

Serves 4

Before sports became a kind of religion in America and its stars our deities, the Indians of the Pacific Northwest considered the salmon a god. It's not uncommon to see sides of salmon crowding out the steaks and burgers outside Qwest Field in Seattle. The great thing about this salmon is that the flavor is so pronounced you don't have to worry about a sauce. Wasabi powder is available in most specialty food shops.

- **¼ cup soy sauce**
- **1 tablespoon dark (Asian) sesame oil**
- **1 tablespoon brown sugar**
- **1 teaspoon ground ginger**
- **1 teaspoon curry powder**
- **¼ to ½ teaspoon wasabi powder, depending on taste**
- **4 salmon fillets, preferably center cut, pinbones removed**
- **Vegetable oil for brushing**
- **2 limes, cut into quarters**

At home In a small, sealable container, mix together the soy sauce, sesame oil, brown sugar, ginger, curry powder, and wasabi powder. Refrigerate until you are ready to pack, up to 24 hours.

At the tailgate Prepare coals for a medium-hot fire.

While the coals are heating, cover the flesh side of the fillets with the soy-wasabi mixture. When the coals are ready, brush the rack with a wad of paper towel dipped in vegetable oil.

Place the salmon fillets on the grill rack, skin side down, and grill for 6 minutes.

Turn and grill until the salmon is just cooked through, 5 to 6 minutes longer. Transfer the salmon to a platter and serve with the limes.

BLACKENED SWORDFISH

Serves 4

This a manly piece of fish, cooked in the now familiar but ever popular Cajun style. The only trick here is not to overcook the steaks. There is only a small window of opportunity to remove the swordfish from the grill when it is perfect. It's about the amount of time the tight end, running a post pattern, is open in the zone between the linebacker and free safety. And you have to find it. You may have to cut into the corner of one of the steaks to see how they're doing, but it's better to do that than to overcook them.

1 teaspoon paprika
1 teaspoon ground black pepper
1 teaspoon onion powder
1 teaspoon garlic powder
1 teaspoon dried thyme
1 teaspoon caraway seeds
½ teaspoon cayenne
½ teaspoon salt
4 swordfish steaks, cut 1 inch thick
2 tablespoons olive oil
Lemon wedges or 1 cup Mango Relish (page 72) 1 for serving

At home In a small, sealable container, mix together the paprika, pepper, onion and garlic powders, thyme, caraway seeds, cayenne, and salt. Set aside until you are ready to pack.

At the tailgate Prepare coals for a medium-hot fire.

While the coals are heating, brush each side of the swordfish steaks with the olive oil. Rub the spice mixture over both sides of each steak.

When the coals are ready, grill the steaks until they are nicely blackened, 5 to 6 minutes. Turn and grill until they are just cooked through, 4 to 5 minutes more. Serve immediately with wedges of fresh lemon or Mango Relish.

GRILLED SHRIMP

Serves 6

Get extra-large shrimp, 16 to 20 per pound being the perfect size for the grill. I made these once for a little tailgate gathering we were having before an outdoor concert. We were with the family of a famous chef. I won't mention his name, because his own kids said these shrimp were better than anything he made that day. Or that week.

- **4 cloves garlic**
- **1 tablespoon coarse salt**
- **2 tablespoons olive oil**
- **2 tablespoons butter, melted**
- **1 teaspoon paprika**
- **1 teaspoon chili powder**
- **½ teaspoon cayenne**
- **36 extra-large shrimp, shelled and deveined**

At home Put the garlic and salt on a cutting board and chop them together. Then use the side of the knife to mash the garlic and salt into a kind of paste. Transfer it to a small bowl and mix in the olive oil, butter, paprika, chili powder, and cayenne.

Put the shrimp in a medium bowl and add the garlic mixture, making sure all the shrimp are completely coated. Transfer to a resealable freezer bag and refrigerate until you are ready to pack, up to 4 hours.

At the tailgate Prepare coals for a very hot fire.

While the coals are heating, thread the shrimp onto skewers, being careful not to crowd them.

When the coals are ready, grill the shrimp until they are opaque in the center, 2 to 3 minutes per side. Serve immediately, though they still rock at room temperature.

Note If using wooden skewers, soak them in water for 1 hour before using to keep them from burning during grilling.

★ ★ ★

SOFT-SHELL CRABS

Serves 4

Soft-shell crabs are available in the spring. Not a lot of football is played in the spring. So if you're not inclined to tailgate baseball, or if that option is not available to you, here's what you should do—Zen tailgate. Go to a park where games are played—you probably pass one every day—bring your grill, and tailgate whatever you find. Maybe it's two teams of 12-year-old girls playing soccer. Maybe it's T-ball. Maybe it's a Babe Ruth league baseball game. Pick a side and root for them because of the color of their uniform. Or better yet, don't root for either team, just enjoy the spirit of athleticism, and the smiles on the kids' faces (ignore the parents altogether, by the way). The soft-shell crabs are the perfect accompaniment to the spirit of this kind of sublime afternoon.

8 soft-shell crabs, cleaned
2 tablespoons olive oil
Salt and ground black pepper
Lemon or lime wedges for serving

At the tailgate Prepare coals for a medium-hot fire. When the coals are ready, brush both sides of the crabs with the olive oil, sprinkle with salt and pepper, and grill until they are golden brown, 5 to 7 minutes, turning once.

Serve with a sprinkling of fresh lemon or lime.

★ ★ ★

CRAB CAKES WITH LIME DRESSING

Serves 4

Dover International Speedway, known as the Miracle Mile, is in Delaware, which is known for its crabs. Usually they're served whole from a bucket, with every diner getting his or her own wooden hammer to crack the shells. And while it's a memorable experience, it's not the easiest mode of dining at a tailgate. Here's another solution, a way to get your crab and eat it, too.

LIME DRESSING

- **3 tablespoons mayonnaise**
- **2 tablespoons sour cream**
- **1 teaspoon Old Bay seasoning**
- **2 teaspoons fresh lime juice**
- **Several dashes of hot sauce**

CRAB CAKES

- **1 pound lump crabmeat, picked over to remove any cartilage or shell**
- **2 tablespoons fresh lemon juice**
- **1 egg**
- **¼ cup plain bread crumbs**
- **2 tablespoons finely chopped scallions, green parts only**
- **2 tablespoons finely chopped fresh parsley**
- **1 tablespoon mayonnaise**
- **1 teaspoon salt**
- **½ teaspoon Dijon mustard**
- **½ teaspoon cayenne**
- **½ cup yellow cornmeal**
- **¼ cup olive oil**

At home **For the lime dressing:** Mix together the mayonnaise, sour cream, Old Bay seasoning, lime juice, and hot sauce. Refrigerate in a sealable container for up to 2 days.

For the crab cakes: In a medium bowl, gently mix together the crabmeat, lemon juice, egg, bread crumbs, scallions, parsley, mayonnaise, salt, mustard, and cayenne, being careful not to break up the lumps of crabmeat.

Shape the mixture into 4 patties and arrange in a sealable container. Refrigerate for at least 1 hour and up to 12 hours.

At the tailgate Prepare coals for a hot fire.

While the coals are heating, place the cornmeal in a pie plate and lay the crab cakes in the cornmeal to coat on both sides.

When the coals are ready, place a medium skillet, preferably cast iron, on the grill rack and let it get hot. Add the olive oil and let it get hot, about 1 minute. Arrange the crab cakes in the skillet and cook until they are nicely browned on the bottom, about 3 minutes. Turn and cook for about 3 minutes more.

Serve immediately with the dressing.

Burgers and Brats

Burgers are ubiquitous among tailgaters. Lurking in the shadows of richly seasoned gumbos and spicy grilled shrimp are grills filled with sizzling burgers, eager tailgaters hovering about, with no concern that they are betraying their local cuisine. That's because in America, burgers belong everywhere.

I find it best to bring the chopped meat en masse to the tailgate and shape it into burgers just before cooking. I've discovered the hard way that it's easy for the burgers to lose their burger shape during transport. You open the cooler to find the meat has reincorporated itself back into one single mass, much like the T-1000 in *Terminator 2*. If you do make your burgers in advance, pack them no more than two high in a sturdy plastic container, with wax paper between layers.

Unlike other meats, even steak, burgers do not do well sitting around after they are cooked. It behooves you to have all the condiments and buns set out and then to rally the troops before the burgers come off the grill. Like a cheap horror-movie effect, even 10 minutes away from the grill can transform a sublime and juicy burger into something dry and less than desirable.

Cooking brats and other sausages is easy, but not simple. The most important thing to remember is to cook them over a medium fire. Any hotter and the brats will burn and split and get ugly. If you can, find a butcher or specialty shop that makes their own sausages. If you live in Wisconsin, this, of course, will be easy. You might even live above one. If you live in Baton Rouge, it might be more problematic. There are quite a few flavors of brat, featuring different spice combinations. Try a few of them. Also keep in mind that standard packaged hot dog rolls will not accommodate a brat's girth, so you need special buns or some hard kaiser rolls.

★ ★ ★

THE BASIC BURGER

Serves 4

When I think of burgers, I think of players like Jim Brown, Al Kaline, Harmon Killebrew, and Rosey Greer. All great players, but men who went about their business without fanfare, without calling attention to their accomplishments. It's the same with a great burger.

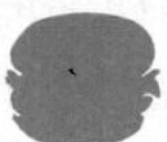

1½ pounds ground round
Salt
4 hamburger buns
Condiments of your choice for serving

At the tailgate Gently shape the meat into 4 burgers about ¾ inch thick and 4½ inches across, handling the meat as little as possible. Make a ¼-inch dent in the center of each burger about the size of a half-dollar with the tips of your middle 3 fingers. Sprinkle both sides with salt.

Prepare coals for a medium-hot fire. When the coals are ready, grill the burgers on one side for 4 minutes. Turn and cook for about 4 minutes more for medium-rare, 5 minutes more for medium. Serve immediately with buns and the condiments of your choice.

★ ★ ★

TACO BURGERS

Serves 4

Kids will especially like these burgers. As a result, you can also use them as a training device to motivate your progeny to become more deeply dedicated to the home team. While you're grilling the burgers, ask the kids the trivia questions they were supposed to study the night before, making sure they know there won't be any burgers for them unless they get a good score. You'll see how fast they remember who holds the school record for yards gained or the most touchdown receptions.

1½ pounds ground round
1 egg
1 can (4 ounces) diced green chiles, drained
2 tablespoons salsa
2 tablespoons finely chopped onion
¼ cup crushed tortilla chips
1 clove garlic, finely chopped
1 teaspoon chili powder
4 hamburger buns
1 cup grated Cheddar cheese
1 cup shredded lettuce
Taco sauce for serving

At home In a large bowl, combine the meat, egg, chiles, salsa, onion, tortilla chips, garlic, and chili powder and mix together with your hands until just combined. Transfer the meat mixture to a resealable freezer bag and refrigerate until you are ready to pack, up to 24 hours.

At the tailgate Gently shape the meat into 4 burgers about ¾ inch thick and 4½ inches across. Make a ¼-inch dent in the center of each burger about the size of a half-dollar with the tips of your middle 3 fingers.

Prepare coals for a medium-hot fire. When the coals are ready, grill the burgers on one side for 4 minutes. Turn and cook for about 4 minutes more for medium-rare, 5 minutes more for medium. Serve immediately in the buns, topped with the cheese, lettuce, and taco sauce.

LAMB, SPINACH, AND MOZZARELLA BURGERS

Serves 4

Here's a nice change from beef burgers. They're a little more exotic, with the currants providing a touch of sweetness and the hidden bits of cheese some added surprise.

¼ cup dried currants
1 tablespoon olive oil
5 cups spinach leaves (about 5 ounces), washed
1¼ pounds ground lamb
3 ounces mozzarella cheese, cut into ½-inch cubes
1 teaspoon ground cumin
1 teaspoon salt
½ teaspoon ground black pepper
4 pita breads
½ cup Cumin Yogurt Dressing (page 145)

At home Soak the currants in hot water to cover for 5 minutes, then drain.

Place a small skillet over medium-high heat and let it get hot, about 2 minutes. Add the olive oil and spread it evenly over the pan. Add the spinach and cook, stirring continuously, until it is wilted, about 4 minutes. Transfer to a plate to cool.

Place the lamb in a medium bowl. Add the spinach, currants, mozzarella cubes, and cumin and mix together by hand until combined. Transfer the meat to a resealable freezer bag and refrigerate until you are ready to pack, up to 24 hours.

At the tailgate Prepare coals for a medium-hot fire. When the coals are ready, grill the burgers for 5 minutes on one side. Turn and grill 5 minutes more for medium. Serve in the pita breads, topped with the dressing.

SALMON BURGERS

Serves 4

These are for non-beef-eaters who still want to have the burger experience. They may be the ones who, while they are watching the game, are heard to exclaim, "Why did he have to tackle him so hard—he didn't even have the ball!?" To which the only answer is a discreet sigh.

1 pound salmon fillet
4 scallions, green parts only, cut into 1-inch pieces
4 cloves garlic, coarsely chopped
2 tablespoons finely chopped fresh ginger
2 tablespoons soy sauce
1 tablespoon dark (Asian) sesame oil
¼ cup bread crumbs
2 tablespoons sesame seeds
2 tablespoons olive oil
4 hamburger buns or pita breads
Lettuce for serving
Bottled Asian sweet chili sauce for serving

At home Remove the skin and any bones from the salmon and cut it into 2-inch chunks.

Place the salmon along with the scallions, garlic, ginger, soy sauce, and sesame oil in the bowl of a food processor fitted with a steel blade and pulse until just combined. Transfer to a medium bowl and add the bread crumbs and sesame seeds and stir to combine.

Shape the mixture into 4 burgers and arrange them in a sealable container big enough to hold them without touching. Refrigerate until you are ready to pack, up to 4 hours.

At the tailgate Prepare coals for a medium fire. When the coals are ready, brush each side of the burgers with the olive oil and grill, turning once, until they are cooked through, 8 to 10 minutes. Serve on buns or in pita breads, topped with lettuce and sweet chili sauce.

★ ★ ★

BRATS LAMBEAU STYLE

Serves 6

This is the way they cook their brats at Lambeau Field, where the Packers play football. If you personally have a different way to cook brats, I strongly suggest you do it somewhere else.

- **2 cans beer**
- **1 large onion, sliced**
- **6 to 12 bratwursts, depending on how many your crowd eats**
- **6 to 12 buns, depending on how many brats you cook**
- **Mustard for serving**
- **1 pound sauerkraut**

At home Place the beer, onion, and brats in a saucepan just big enough to hold them. Bring to a boil over medium-high heat, then reduce the heat to low and simmer until the brats are just cooked through, about 8 minutes. Remove the pan from the heat and let the brats cool in the liquid.

Transfer the brats and their cooking liquid to a sealable container and refrigerate until you are ready to pack, up to 24 hours. Then clean out the pan. You're going to bring it with you.

At the tailgate Prepare coals for a medium fire. When the coals are ready, lay the brats on the grill. Quickly transfer the cooking liquid to the saucepan and put that on the grill as well to heat up.

Cook the brats for 8 to 10 minutes, turning as needed to get them brown on all sides. Once they are done, return them to the pot with the cooking liquid. Serve them from there with mustard and sauerkraut.

Note It's important to know that the brats for this recipe are *not* precooked. Using those at Lambeau is like eating your brat with ketchup. These are rookie mistakes—you're allowed to screw up one time, unless you cost the team the game.

SMOKED BRAT AND SAUERKRAUT PACKETS

Serves 4

Here's another version of brats. These you will not find in Packer country, because they are precooked. But since most of the people tailgating on any given NFL Sunday are not outside Lambeau Field, you should feel free to give these a try.

- **1 pound smoked bratwursts, cut into 1-inch pieces**
- **8 small red potatoes, cut into ½-inch rounds**
- **2 cups sauerkraut, undrained**
- **¼ cup ketchup**
- **¼ cup coarse, grainy mustard**
- **1 teaspoon caraway seeds**

At home In a medium bowl, mix together the brats, potatoes, sauerkraut, ketchup, mustard, and caraway seeds. Divide the mixture equally among four 12-inch sheets of aluminum foil. Bring the long ends together and fold them tightly several times. Then fold up the sides to make a neat, sealed packet. Refrigerate until you are ready to pack, up to 12 hours.

At the tailgate Prepare coals for a medium fire. When the coals are ready, place the brat and potato packets on the rack and cook for 14 minutes, turning once.

Open the packets carefully to avoid the escaping steam, and serve.

BUD LIGHT
weber
weber

Hail Marys: Chili and Stew

Some games come down to one play. These dishes all come down to one pot. But unlike a long, last-second pass thrown in desperation, these recipes guarantee success.

So here is your main course in one pot, all ready to go. There's something to be said for that kind of reassurance. You've done all the work at home; now it's almost like you're a guest at your own party. You can still fire up the grill, but you're under a lot less pressure, knowing you have a pot of something warm and luxuriantly flavored waiting to be served.

Most chilis and stews benefit from being made the day before. For some reason the flavor intensifies as it sits overnight in the fridge. Maybe it's thinking about the big game, getting pysched, pumping itself up for its glorious moment in the tailgate sun. The easiest way to reheat your chili or stew is on a tabletop burner. You can easily adjust the flame to help keep the bottom from scorching. The other way to reheat is to use the grill. I've had more success reheating on the grill by dividing a big pot of chili into two smaller pots. It takes less time, uses fewer coals, and seems to better keep the bottom from scorching.

Try to get your chili or stew as hot as possible. That way, the rice or noodles you serve it over will be heated through by the chili. I've seen several tailgaters serve their chili or stew in doubled-up paper coffee cups. This seems to keep the chili hot longer on cold days and also helps warm your hands. When you're done, throw away the inside cup and save the clean outside one for mulled cider or hot chocolate.

Note:

All dishes in this section are prepared completely at home and need only be reheated at the tailgate.

CHILI SIMPATICO

Serves 8

This is one of those dishes you can throw together in 15 minutes, which is especially beneficial when the vicissitudes of your weekday life conspire to prevent you from preparing for your tailgate as gloriously as you otherwise might.

- **2 tablespoons vegetable oil**
- **4 pounds ground sirloin**
- **¼ cup chili powder**
- **1 tablespoon ground cumin**
- **1 can (6 ounces) tomato paste**
- **2 cups beef broth**
- **2 cups water**
- **2 medium onions, finely chopped**
- **2 green bell peppers, cored, seeded, and finely chopped**
- **2 tablespoons dried oregano**
- **1 tablespoon garlic powder**
- **Salt**
- **1 cup grated Cheddar or Monterey Jack cheese**

At home Place a large pot over high heat, add the vegetable oil, and let it get hot. When the oil just starts to smoke, add the meat and cook, breaking it up with the back of a spoon, until all the pink is gone, about 5 minutes. Spoon out some of the fat. Add the chili powder and cumin and cook, stirring often, for 1 minute. Add the tomato paste and cook for 1 minute more.

Add the beef broth, water, onions, bell peppers, oregano, garlic powder, and salt to taste and bring the mixture to a boil. Reduce the heat to low, cover, and simmer the chili for 1 hour, stirring every 20 minutes or so to keep the bottom from scorching.

Correct the seasoning and let cool before transferring the chili to a sealable container and refrigerating for up to 3 days.

At the tailgate Reheat the chili and serve topped with a sprinkling of cheese.

TAILGATING TALES

THE NOBLE ONES

Arlene and Ben Roth are die-hard Ohio State Buckeye fans and devout tailgaters. They've been tailgating steadily for the last thirty years. Their van has been customized to be entirely scarlet and gray. The covering of their spare tire has an airbrushed portrait of the stadium. The Roths were winners of the Best Buckeye Tailgaters the first and only year the contest was held. They followed the team to the Rose Bowl and tailgated there, at one point helping the Buckeyes' star fullback get from the hotel to the team's practice when he accidentally missed the team bus. The Roths are joined at every game by several friends who help decorate their table and tent with a decades-old collection of team pennants, trinkets, stuffed animals, and mojos. One friend, who has since passed away, is represented by the large pennant she would always bring. Arlene and Ben are the leaders of their group, but they rely on others for most of the food. They are especially beholden to their friend Marvin for his chili, which is the mainstay of their party. It's kept warm in a special pot in the corner of one of their grills and is doled out in paper coffee cups, warming up the crowd come November when Columbus mornings get nippy. Marvin, like most great chili creators, refuses to give up his recipe, but fans of Marvin's chili say it is distinguished by having a little of everything in it. The Roths hope to be tailgating for a long time to come, and in so many ways they represent the best aspects of this uniquely American tradition.

★ ★ ★

CHILI CON TODO

Serves 8

This chili has everything you want in chili and then some. And then some more after that. You can do what the Roths do on particularly cold days, which is to have the chili ready early so people can nosh on it whenever they want something to warm them up.

- **6 slices bacon, cut into 1-inch pieces**
- **1 pound pork tenderloin, cut into 1-inch cubes**
- **2 medium onions, finely chopped**
- **2 poblano chiles, stemmed, seeded, and finely chopped**
- **6 cloves garlic, finely chopped**
- **1 pound ground sirloin**
- **¼ cup chili powder**
- **2 tablespoons ground cumin**
- **1 can (6 ounces) tomato paste**
- **2 cans (4 ounces each) diced green chiles, drained**
- **1 can (4 ounces) diced jalapeño chiles, drained**
- **4 cups water**
- **1 can (28 ounces) crushed tomatoes**
- **1 cup coarsely chopped pitted green olives**
- **1 teaspoon ground cinnamon**
- **2 tablespoons dried oregano**
- **1 can (12 ounces) pinto beans, drained**
- **1 can (12 ounces) black beans, drained**
- **1 package (12 ounces) frozen corn**

At home Place a large pot over medium-high heat and add the bacon. When it has rendered most of its fat, remove with a slotted spoon and set aside on paper towels. Pour off most of the bacon fat and return the pot to the heat.

Raise the heat to high and add the pork. Cook until browned, about 5 minutes. Remove the pork with a slotted spoon and set aside.

Return the pot to the heat, add the onions and poblano chiles, and cook until the onions soften, about 5 minutes. Add the garlic and cook for 1 minute more. Add the ground sirloin and cook, breaking up the meat, until all the pink is gone, about 5 minutes more.

Add the chili powder and cumin and cook, stirring often, for 1 minute. Add the tomato paste and cook for 1 minute more.

Crumble the cooked bacon and add to the pot, along with the green chiles, jalapeños, water, tomatoes, olives, cinnamon, and oregano and bring the mixture to a boil. Reduce the heat to medium-low, cover, and simmer the chili for 1 hour, stirring every 20 minutes or so to keep the bottom from scorching.

Add the pinto beans, black beans, and corn and simmer for 20 minutes more, stirring often. Let cool and transfer to a sealable container. Refrigerate for up to 3 days.

At the tailgate Reheat the chili and serve.

★ ★ ★

CINCINNATI BENGAL CHILI

Serves 6

The parking lot of Paul Brown Stadium is where the die-hard Bengals fans do their tailgating. The distinctive aroma of Cincinnati chili, awash with bay leaves and a touch of cinnamon, wafts over the crowd. It is, however, the fierce devotion to pasta on the bottom and Cheddar cheese and chopped onion on top ("three way" style) that links this chili unmistakably to Bengal country.

2 tablespoons butter
2 medium onions, finely chopped
6 cloves garlic, finely chopped
2 pounds ground sirloin
¼ cup chili powder
1 teaspoon unsweetened cocoa powder
1 teaspoon ground cinnamon
1 teaspoon ground allspice
1 teaspoon ground cumin
2 cups water
4 bay leaves
2 tablespoons cider vinegar
2 tablespoons honey
1 can (12 ounces) red kidney beans, drained
1 pound elbow macaroni, cooked
2 cups grated sharp Cheddar cheese
1 cup diced red onion

At home Place a large pot over medium heat. Add the butter and the onions and cook, stirring often, until the onions soften, about 5 minutes. Add the garlic and cook for 2 minutes more.

Increase the heat to high and add the meat. Cook until it loses its pinkness, about 6 minutes, stirring frequently and breaking the meat up with the back of a spoon.

Add the chili powder, cocoa powder, cinnamon, allspice, and cumin and cook for 2 minutes, stirring frequently.

Add the water, bay leaves, vinegar, and honey and bring the mixture to a boil. Reduce the heat to low and simmer, covered, for 45 minutes, stirring occasionally to keep the bottom from scorching.

Add the beans and cook for 15 minutes more. Let cool and transfer to a sealable container. Refrigerate for up to 3 days.

At the tailgate Reheat the chili. Serve in bowls over the elbow macaroni. Top with a generous helping of the cheese and diced onion.

Note To make the macaroni easier to transport to the tailgate, toss the cooled cooked macaroni lightly in olive oil before placing it in a resealable plastic bag. Refrigerate until ready to pack.

★ ★ ★

VENISON CHILI

Serves 6

Some say the other official color in Green Bay, besides Packers green and gold, is orange. It's what hunters wear so they don't get shot by other hunters, or at least not with any frequency. Since deer season overlaps with football season, it's no accident that there's a lot of venison available, and that's why this chili is another popular dish outside Lambeau Field. This preparation uses less tomato than other versions and is slightly thicker, to better feature the distinctive flavor of the venison. Add some water or beef broth to the pot when reheating.

4 tablespoons vegetable oil
1½ pounds ground venison
1 medium onion, finely chopped
4 cloves garlic, finely chopped
1 tablespoon chili powder
1 tablespoon dried oregano
½ teaspoon ground cinnamon
1 can (15 ounces) crushed tomatoes
1 can (12 ounces) pinto beans, drained
1 cup beef broth
1 teaspoon salt
1 teaspoon ground black pepper

At home Place a large pot over medium-high heat, add 2 tablespoons of the vegetable oil and the venison and cook until the meat is no longer pink, about 6 minutes. Transfer the venison to a bowl, return the pot to the heat, add the remaining oil and the onion and cook, stirring often, until the onion is soft, about 8 minutes. Add the garlic and cook for 1 minute more.

Add the chili powder, oregano, and cinnamon and cook for 1 minute more, stirring continuously.

Return the venison to the pot and add the tomatoes, beans, beef broth, salt, and pepper. Raise the heat to high and bring the mixture to a boil. Immediately reduce the heat to low, cover, and simmer the chili for 45 minutes, stirring every 10 minutes to keep it from scorching.

Let cool and transfer to a sealable container. Refrigerate for up to 3 days.

At the tailgate Reheat the chili and serve.

BEEF STEW

Serves 6

A lot of us have forgotten how great a simple, old-fashioned beef stew can be. But on a crisp autumn afternoon, this is the perfect way to keep warm.

- **4** ounces slab bacon, cut into 1-inch pieces
- **2 to 2½** pounds beef chuck or round, trimmed and cut into 1- to 1½-inch cubes
- **1** tablespoon olive oil
- **2** large onions, cut in half lengthwise and then into ¼-inch slices
- **2** teaspoons sugar
- **3** tablespoons unbleached all-purpose flour
- **2** cups chicken broth
- **1** cup red wine
- **3** tablespoons tomato paste
- **6** cloves garlic, coarsely chopped
- **1** bay leaf
- **1** teaspoon fresh thyme leaves, or ½ teaspoon dried thyme
- **4** medium potatoes, peeled and cut into 1-inch pieces
- **4** carrots, peeled and cut into 1-inch pieces
- **4** small white turnips, cut into 1-inch pieces
- **1** package (12 ounces) frozen peas
- Salt and ground black pepper

At home Place a medium pot (preferably a Dutch oven) over medium-high heat, add the bacon and cook, stirring frequently, until it is crisp. Remove with a slotted spoon and pour out the excess fat.

Brown half the beef in the remaining bacon fat, being careful not to crowd it or it will not brown properly. Transfer to a platter and repeat with the remaining beef.

Add the olive oil to the pot along with the onions and cook, stirring frequently, until they soften, about 8 minutes. Add the sugar and cook for 1 minute more, stirring continuously. Add the flour and cook for 2 minutes more, stirring continuously.

Return the beef to the pot, along with the chicken broth, wine, tomato paste, garlic, bay leaf, and thyme and bring the mixture to a boil. Immediately reduce the heat to low, cover the pot, and simmer for 30 minutes.

Add the potatoes, carrots, and turnips and simmer, covered, for 45 minutes more.

Add the peas and cooked bacon and cook for 5 minutes more. Let the stew cool and transfer to a sealable container. Refrigerate for up to 48 hours.

At the tailgate Reheat the stew and serve.

★ ★ ★

BURGOO

Serves 8

The first NASCAR race was run in 1948 on the beach track at Daytona, Florida. But stock car racing has its roots in North Carolina and Virginia, where Junior Johnson and his fellow moonshiners souped up their cars to outrun the police. Burgoo is a traditional stew that hails from this region. It was traditionally made with small game such as rabbit, possum, or squirrel. Feel free to substitute squirrel for the chicken thighs.

- **1 pound lamb shoulder roast, cut into 1-inch cubes**
- **8 ounces pork butt, cut into 1-inch cubes**
- **4 cups beef broth**
- **4 cups chicken broth**
- **1½ pounds chicken thighs**
- **2 pounds potatoes, peeled and diced**
- **1 medium red onion, diced**
- **1 package (12 ounces) frozen fava or lima beans**
- **1 green bell pepper, cored, seeded, and coarsely chopped**
- **3 carrots, peeled and coarsely chopped**
- **1 package (12 ounces) frozen corn**
- **2 dried ancho chiles, stemmed, seeded, and chopped into ½-inch pieces**
- **½ teaspoon cayenne**
- **1½ teaspoons kosher salt**
- **1 teaspoon ground black pepper**
- **1 can (28 ounces) chopped tomatoes**
- **4 cloves garlic, finely chopped**
- **2 teaspoons cider vinegar**
- **2 teaspoons fresh lemon juice**
- **3 tablespoons bourbon**
- **3 tablespoons Worcestershire sauce**
- **1 tablespoon hot sauce**
- **½ cup chopped fresh parsley**

At home In a large pot, combine the lamb and pork with the beef and chicken broths. Bring to a boil, then reduce the heat to low and simmer for 1 hour. Add the chicken thighs and simmer for 1 hour more. Remove the chicken from the pot and let cool slightly.

Remove the skin and bones, shred the meat, and return it to the pot. Add the potatoes, onion, fava beans, bell pepper, carrots, corn, ancho chiles, cayenne, salt, and pepper and simmer for 1 hour more.

Add the tomatoes, garlic, vinegar, lemon juice, bourbon, Worcestershire sauce, and hot sauce and simmer for 1 hour more. Let cool and transfer to a sealable container. Refrigerate until you are ready to pack, up to 24 hours.

At the tailgate Reheat the burgoo, stir in the parsley, and serve.

★ ★ ★

SHRIMP AND CHICKEN JAMBALAYA

Serves 4

You can never make jambalaya as good as that Other Guy, the one with the reputation for the best jambalaya in the parking lot, who's got some secret maneuvers and nifty jambalaya jukes that no one else can duplicate. Still, you can try. And who knows, after a few successful attempts using this recipe, maybe someday *you* will be the Other Guy, and, lured by the aroma and your reputation, people will stop by your tailgate party, humbly, plate in hand, hoping for a taste.

- **2 tablespoons vegetable oil**
- **1 pound skinless, boneless chicken thighs, cut into 1-inch pieces**
- **8 ounces andouille sausage, cut into ½-inch pieces**
- **1 medium onion, finely chopped**
- **3 stalks celery, finely chopped**
- **1 green bell pepper, cored, seeded, and finely chopped**
- **6 scallions, green parts only, finely chopped**
- **4 cloves garlic, finely chopped**
- **2 bay leaves**
- **2 teaspoons dried oregano**
- **2 teaspoons ground black pepper**
- **1 teaspoon dried thyme**
- **1½ teaspoons salt**
- **1 teaspoon cayenne**
- **1 can (28 ounces) crushed tomatoes**
- **1 can (8 ounces) clams with juice**
- **2 cups chicken broth**
- **1 pound large shrimp, shelled and deveined**
- **2 cups cooked white rice**

At home Place a large pot, preferably a Dutch oven, over high heat and let it get very hot, about 2 minutes. Add the vegetable oil and spread it evenly over the pot. Add the chicken and cook until it is browned, about 5 minutes. Remove the chicken with a slotted spoon and set aside. Add the sausage and cook until it is crispy, about 5 minutes. Add the onion, celery, bell pepper, and scallions and cook until the vegetables are soft, about 8 minutes. Add the garlic and cook for 1 minute more. Return the chicken to the pot along with the bay leaves, oregano, pepper, thyme, salt, and cayenne and cook for 1 minute more, stirring continuously.

Add the tomatoes, clams with the liquid, and chicken broth. Bring to a boil, then reduce the heat and simmer for 20 minutes. Let cool. The jambalaya can be prepared to this point up to 24 hours before serving. Transfer to a sealable container and refrigerate.

At the tailgate Prepare coals for a medium fire. When the coals are ready, place a large skillet with the chicken mixture on the grill. Add the shrimp, cover the pan with aluminum foil, then cover the grill and cook, stirring occasionally, for 12 minutes. Add the cooked rice and cook for 5 minutes more.

TAILGATE GUMBO

Serves 6

While the LSU marching band is warming up before the game in the Huey Long Greek Amphitheater, LSU Tiger fans are warming up pots of gumbo. Someone may need to stay and stir while the rest of the group lines the path the team takes as they walk from their dorms to the stadium. Many LSU games are played at night, which gives tailgaters time to prepare their gumbo the morning of the game. Unlike chili, gumbo is best served the day it is made.

- **6 tablespoons vegetable oil**
- **2 pounds boneless, skinless chicken thighs, cut into 1-inch pieces**
- **1 pound andouille sausage, cut into ½-inch pieces**
- **6 cups chicken broth**
- **½ cup unbleached all-purpose flour**
- **4 stalks celery, finely chopped**
- **1 large onion, finely chopped**
- **1 green bell pepper, cored, seeded, and finely chopped**
- **6 scallions, green parts only, finely chopped**
- **4 cloves garlic, finely chopped**
- **1 package (10 ounces) frozen cut okra, thawed**
- **2 tablespoons tomato paste**
- **2 bay leaves**
- **1 tablespoon dried thyme**
- **1 teaspoon Tabasco or other hot sauce**
- **1 teaspoon sweet paprika**
- **½ teaspoon ground allspice**
- **Salt and ground black pepper**
- **1 pound extra-large shrimp, shelled and deveined**
- **2 cups cooked white rice**

At home Place a skillet, preferably cast iron, over high heat and let it get hot. Add 2 tablespoons of the vegetable oil and half the chicken thigh pieces and brown on all sides, about 6 minutes. Transfer to a large bowl. Add the remaining chicken to the skillet, brown, and transfer to the bowl.

Return the pan to the heat, add the sausage, and cook until it is brown, about 6 minutes. Transfer the sausage to the bowl with the chicken, and clean and dry the skillet.

Slowly heat the chicken broth in a medium pot over low heat.

While the broth is heating, make the roux. Place the skillet over medium-low heat, add the remaining 4 tablespoons oil and the flour and cook, whisking continuously, until the mixture becomes a deep, rich reddish brown, 20 to 25 minutes. (This is a good time to listen to your local sports radio station for the skinny on the big game.)

Add the celery, onion, bell pepper, scallions, and garlic to the roux and cook, stirring frequently, until the vegetables soften, about 8 minutes.

Slowly add 1 cup of the hot broth to the roux and stir to incorporate. Carefully transfer the roux mixture into the pot with the broth and stir to combine. Add the browned chicken and sausage along with the okra, tomato paste, bay leaves, thyme, Tabasco, paprika, allspice, and salt and pepper to taste. Bring to a boil over medium-high heat, then immediately turn the heat down to medium-low and simmer, uncovered, for 45 minutes. Add the shrimp and simmer until they are cooked through, about 6 minutes more. Remove from the heat and let cool. Transfer to a sealable container and refrigerate until you are ready to pack, up to 24 hours.

At the tailgate Reheat the gumbo and serve in bowls over the rice.

ISLAND STEW

Serves 4

Believe it or not, New York City is one of the hotbeds of cricket in the United States. There are several tournaments each year, including the most prestigious prize in American cricket, the New York Caribbean Cricket Cup. If tailgating cricket matches catches on, you might see this dish make an appearance. Meanwhile, it can bring a bit of Island spice to your party.

- **4 tablespoons vegetable oil**
- **2 pounds boneless, skinless chicken thighs, cut into 1-inch cubes**
- **1 pound boneless pork, cut into 1-inch cubes**
- **1 leek, white part only, thinly sliced**
- **1 large red onion, finely chopped**
- **8 ounces audouille sausage, cut into ½-inch slices**
- **¼ cup finely chopped garlic**
- **3 tablespoons finely chopped fresh ginger**
- **2 tablespoons brown sugar**
- **1 teaspoon ground allspice**
- **1½ pounds sweet potato, peeled and cut into 1-inch cubes**
- **1 jalapeño chile, stemmed, seeded, and finely chopped**
- **2 bay leaves**
- **1 cinnamon stick, 3 inches long**
- **1 cup chicken broth**
- **2 cups cooked white rice**

At home Place a medium, heavy-bottomed pot (preferably a Dutch oven) over high heat. Add 2 tablespoons of the vegetable oil and the chicken and cook until the chicken is nicely browned on all sides, about 5 minutes. Remove the chicken to a platter.

Add another tablespoon of the oil to the pot along with the pork and cook until the pork is nicely browned on all sides, about 5 minutes. Transfer to the platter with the chicken.

Pour off any excess fat and add the remaining tablespoon of oil along with the leek and onion and cook for 5 minutes. Add the sausage, garlic, and ginger and cook for 2 minutes more, stirring frequently. Add the brown sugar and allspice and cook for 1 minute more, stirring continuously.

Add the sweet potato, jalapeño, bay leaves, cinnamon stick, and chicken broth, along with the chicken and pork, and bring the mixture to a boil. Reduce the heat to low, cover the pot, and simmer for 1 hour.

Remove the cinnamon stick and let cool. Transfer to to a sealable container and refrigerate until you are ready to pack, up to 24 hours.

At the tailgate Reheat the stew and serve in bowls over the rice.

BOOYAH

Serves 12

The epitome of Green Bay tailgating is to indulge in the Three B's—Brats, Booyah, and Beer—all on the same day. Booyah is an ever-evolving chicken stew that had its origins in Belgium and came to Wisconsin in the 1800s with the settlers. Booyah is not worth making unless you have a crowd. But alert a few people that you're making booyah, and you'll definitely *have* a crowd.

3 pounds chicken thighs
1 pound beef stew meat, such as chuck, with bones
1 pound pork stew meat, with bones
½ cup minced fresh parsley
1 tablespoon salt
1 tablespoon dried rosemary
1 tablespoon dried thyme
½ teaspoon ground black pepper
½ teaspoon dried sage
1½ pounds potatoes, peeled and cut into ½-inch dice
1 large onion, finely chopped
4 celery stalks, coarsely chopped
3 large carrots, coarsely chopped
6 ounces green beans, cut into 1-inch pieces
1 package (12 ounces) frozen peas
1 cup peeled, seeded, chopped tomatoes
2 lemons

At home Put the chicken, beef, and pork in a large pot along with the parsley, salt, rosemary, thyme, pepper, and sage. Cover by about an inch with water and bring to a boil over medium heat. Once the liquid starts boiling, immediately reduce the heat to low, cover, and simmer for 1 hour.

Remove the chicken, re-cover the pot, and let the pork and beef continue simmering for 1 hour longer. Remove the pork and beef from the pot and, when cool enough to handle, remove the meat, including the chicken, from the bones. Cut or pull the meat into 2-inch pieces and return it to the pot.

Add the potatoes, onions, celery, carrots, green beans, peas, and tomatoes to the pot and simmer until the potatoes are just cooked through, about 10 more minutes.

Grate the zest from 1 of the lemons and set aside. Squeeze the juice from both lemons and add it to the pot. Taste for seasoning. Let cool and transfer to a sealable container. Refrigerate until you are ready to pack, up to 24 hours.

At the tailgate Reheat the stew and serve sprinkled with the lemon zest.

★ ★ ★

MEXICAN WEDDING SEAFOOD STEW

Serves 6

Not quite as heavy as a beef stew, this will still warm you up on a cold day.

- **1 can (28 ounces) whole plum tomatoes, drained**
- **1 medium onion, coarsely chopped**
- **3 cloves garlic, coarsely chopped**
- **1 canned chipotle chile in adobo sauce**
- **2 tablespoons olive oil**
- **3 cups chicken broth**
- **1 can (6 ounces) whole clams with juice**
- **1½ pounds sweet potatoes, peeled, sliced lengthwise into quarters, and cut into ½-inch slices**
- **1 cup coarsely chopped fresh cilantro**
- **2 tablespoons chili powder**
- **1 teaspoon ground cumin**
- **1 teaspoon salt**
- **1 pound skinless, boneless firm-fleshed white fish, such as halibut, red snapper, or grouper, cut into 1-inch pieces**
- **1 pound large shrimp, peeled and deveined**
- **Lime wedges for serving**

At home In a blender or food processor, purée the tomatoes, onion, garlic, and chipotle chile and process until it is a smooth paste.

Place a medium pot, preferably a Dutch oven, over medium-high heat, add the olive oil, and let it get very hot, about 2 minutes. Add the purée and cook, stirring, until it thickens to the consistency of ketchup.

Add the chicken broth, clams and their juice, sweet potatoes, cilantro, chili powder, cumin, and salt and bring to a boil. Reduce the heat to low, cover, and simmer until the potatoes are cooked through, about 15 minutes.

Raise the heat to high, and when the mixture starts boiling, add the fish and shrimp. When the mixture returns to a boil, reduce the heat to low and simmer for 10 minutes.

Turn off the heat and correct the seasoning if necessary. Let cool and transfer to a sealable container. Refrigerate until you are ready to pack, up to 24 hours.

At the tailgate Reheat the stew and serve with lime wedges.

Kabob's Your Uncle

Kabobs are one of the great tailgate dishes. They are easy to grill; they happen to fit perfectly on a hibachi; they've got the vegetables already attached; they're already seasoned and ready to cook; and because they are already cut up, they don't require knives, allowing you to eat with one hand and keep the other hand free to hold your beer. You can easily improvise your own kabobs by cutting whatever it is you want to grill into 1-inch pieces and threading them onto skewers. Just remember the following:

★

Soak wooden skewers in water for 30 minutes before using to help keep them from burning on the grill.

★

Use medium or medium-high heat—too hot a fire will wind up scorching the outside of the meat and leaving the inside uncooked. Also keep in mind that although the meat has been cut into smaller pieces, the thickness is still about the same, so the required cooking time will be about the same as well.

★

Invest in a rectangular, sealable plastic container to transport the kabobs in their marinade. A resealable plastic bag won't work, as the points of the skewers will puncture it.

★

Place used skewers in an empty wine or liter soda bottle. That way when you throw them out, they won't pierce your garbage bag, causing unwanted leakage.

★ ★ ★

CURRIED BEEF KABOBS

Serves 4

Tenderloin makes beautiful kabobs. It's a bit pricey, and people can't necessarily see where the money went, as they can with a 2-pound porterhouse, but they'll know once they taste it.

CUMIN YOGURT DRESSING

- **1 cup plain yogurt**
- **¼ cup minced onion**
- **¼ cup finely chopped fresh cilantro, or 1 teaspoon ground coriander**
- **¼ cup finely chopped fresh mint**
- **1 teaspoon ground cumin**
- **½ teaspoon ground ginger**
- **½ teaspoon salt**
- **Pinch of cayenne**

- **½ cup minced onion**
- **3 tablespoons olive oil**
- **2 tablespoons finely chopped garlic**
- **1 tablespoon curry powder**
- **1 teaspoon salt**
- **1 teaspoon ground black pepper**
- **2 pounds beef tenderloin, cut into 1½-inch pieces**
- **8 ounces button mushrooms, stems trimmed**
- **1 large red onion, cut into 1-inch pieces**

At home **For the cumin yogurt dressing:** In a medium sealable container, mix together the yogurt, onion, cilantro, mint, cumin, ginger, salt, and cayenne. Store in the refrigerator until ready to serve. The dressing will keep for up to 5 days, its flavor intensifying a bit. Allow it to come to room temperature before serving.

In a small bowl, mix together the minced onion, olive oil, garlic, curry powder, salt, and pepper. Thread the pieces of beef onto 8 skewers, alternating with the mushrooms and red onion. Place the skewers in a sealable container just large enough to hold them and pour the onion mixture over them, making sure all sides of the kabobs are coated. Refrigerate until you are ready to pack, up to 4 hours.

At the tailgate Prepare coals for a medium-hot fire. When the coals are ready, grill the kabobs for 6 to 7 minutes for medium-rare, turning several times to cook all sides.

Serve immediately with the dressing.

★★★

HAWAIIAN CHICKEN KABOBS

Serves 4

The Pro Bowl, played in Hawaii, is a reward for those players who are the best in the league at their positions. However masterful you are at tailgating, though, it's unlikely that anyone is going to pick up the tab to send you to Hawaii to tailgate the Pro Bowl. This dish at least offers a taste of the islands, so you can celebrate a season when you put up career tailgating numbers.

- ½ **cup frozen orange juice concentrate, thawed**
- ¼ **cup honey**
- ¼ **cup soy sauce**
- 2 **teaspoons curry powder**
- 1 **teaspoon ground ginger**
- 4 **boneless, skinless chicken breasts, cut into 1½-inch pieces**
- 1 **red bell pepper, cored, seeded, and cut into 1-inch pieces**
- 1 **can pineapple chunks, drained**

At home In a small bowl, mix together the orange juice, honey, soy sauce, curry powder, and ginger. Alternately thread pieces of chicken, bell pepper, and pineapple onto 8 skewers. Place the skewers in a sealable container just large enough to hold them, and pour the sauce over them, making sure all sides of the kabobs are coated. Refrigerate until you are ready to pack, up to 4 hours.

At the tailgate Prepare coals for a medium-hot fire. When the coals are ready, grill the kabobs for 8 to 10 minutes, basting with the sauce and turning several times to cook all sides, until the chicken is just cooked through. Serve immediately.

SOUTHWESTERN CHICKEN KABOBS

Serves 4

I like to prepare these kabobs to take to the tailgate along with some steaks or chops. They appeal to non-meat-eaters but are substantial enough that they won't be overwhelmed on the serving table by the platter of steaks.

½ cup olive oil
6 cloves garlic, finely chopped
¼ cup finely chopped fresh cilantro
¼ cup finely chopped fresh mint
2 canned chipotle chiles in adobo sauce, finely chopped
1 tablespoon chili powder
2 teaspoons ground cumin
1 jalapeño chile, stemmed, seeded, and finely chopped
1 teaspoon salt
1½ pounds skinless, boneless chicken breasts or thighs, cut into 1½-inch pieces
1 large sweet onion, peeled and cut into ½-inch pieces
1 red bell pepper, cored, seeded, and cut into 1-inch squares
3 small zucchini, cut into 1-inch rounds

At home In a medium bowl, mix together the ½ cup olive oil, the garlic, cilantro, mint, chipotle chiles, chili powder, cumin, jalapeño, and the salt. Alternately thread the chicken and vegetable pieces onto 8 skewers. Place the skewers in a sealable container just large enough to hold them, and pour any remaining marinade over them. Refrigerate until you are ready to pack, up to 4 hours.

At the tailgate Prepare coals for medium-hot fire.

When the coals are ready, grill the kabobs for 8 to 10 minutes for breasts, 10 to 12 minutes for thighs, turning each skewer a quarter turn every 2 or 2½ minutes, until the meat is no longer pink in the center. Serve immediately.

★ ★ ★

JERK CHICKEN KABOBS

Serves 4

Everyone needs a little jerk flavor now and again. The fiery taste of Scotch bonnet peppers adds the kind of jolt you may need to break down your inhibitions and start expressing your team spirit. Make sure you know the cheers before you're ready to shout them, though often a ferocious exclamation of any three vowels of your choosing will be enough to establish your deeply felt fealty to the team.

JERK MARINADE

- **¼ cup hot sauce made from Scotch bonnet peppers**
- **4 scallions, green parts only, roughly cut into 3-inch lengths**
- **2 cloves garlic, mashed**
- **¼ cup packed fresh parsley leaves**
- **¼ cup fresh orange juice**
- **¼ cup fresh lime juice (from about 2 large limes)**
- **3 tablespoons Dijon mustard**
- **2 tablespoons white vinegar**
- **1 teaspoon salt**
- **½ teaspoon dried rosemary**
- **½ teaspoon ground allspice**
- **½ teaspoon ground cinnamon**

- **2 pounds boneless, skinless chicken breasts or thighs, cut into 1½-inch cubes**
- **2 red bell peppers, cored, seeded, and cut into 1-inch squares**
- **1 medium red onion, cut into 1-inch pieces**

At home **For the jerk marinade:** Place the hot sauce, scallions, garlic, parsley, orange juice, lime juice, mustard, vinegar, salt, rosemary, allspice, and cinnamon in a blender and pulse until the mixture becomes a smooth paste.

Alternately thread pieces of chicken, bell pepper, and onion onto 8 skewers. Place the skewers in a sealable container just large enough to hold them and pour the jerk marinade over them, making sure all sides of the kabobs are coated. Refrigerate until you are ready to pack, up to 4 hours.

At the tailgate Prepare coals for a medium-hot fire. When the coals are ready, grill the kabobs for 8 to 10 minutes for breasts, 10 to 12 minutes for thighs, turning each skewer a quarter turn every 2 or 2½ minutes, until the meat is no longer pink in the center. Serve immediately.

★ ★ ★

PROSCIUTTO-WRAPPED PORK KABOBS

Serves 4

A quick way to liven up pork tenderloins is to infuse them with the sweet, cured flavor of the prosciutto.

2 pork tenderloins, cut into 1½-inch pieces
8 ounces thinly sliced prosciutto
1 large sweet onion, cut into ½-inch pieces
1 red bell pepper, cored, seeded, and cut into 1-inch squares
2 large portobello mushrooms, dark gills scraped away, cut into 1-inch pieces
2 tablespoons olive oil

At home Wrap each piece of pork in enough prosciutto to cover it. Alternately thread the proscuitto-wrapped pork with the vegetable pieces onto 8 skewers. Transfer to a sealable container just large enough to hold them and refrigerate until you are ready to pack, up to 4 hours.

At the tailgate Prepare coals for a medium fire. When the coals are ready, brush the kabobs with the olive oil and grill for 12 minutes, turning each skewer a quarter turn every 3 minutes, until the pork is no longer pink in the center. Serve immediately.

Note Because you are cooking the prosciutto, you need not purchase the most expensive imported Italian product. A good-quality domestic prosciutto will work fine.

igloo COOL

★ ★ ★

ITALIAN SAUSAGE AND FENNEL KABOBS

Serves 4

The pairing of the fennel and sausage brings a little taste of Sicily to your party. Simmering the sausages before you set out for your tailgating means they will need only a short time on the grill, making for more expedient cooking.

- **1 pound sweet or hot Italian sausages**
- **2 bulbs fennel, tops trimmed**
- **2 cups white wine**
- **1 teaspoon fennel seeds**
- **1 teaspoon dried oregano**
- **2 portobello mushrooms, dark gills scraped away, cut in half and then into 1-inch slices**
- **2 tablespoons olive oil**
- **2 tablespoons balsamic vinegar**

At home With a fork, pierce the sausages in several places. Quarter the fennel bulbs lengthwise. Place the sausages and the fennel in a medium saucepan. Add the wine, fennel seeds, and oregano and bring to a boil. Immediately reduce the heat to low and simmer for about 8 minutes.

Remove the sausages and fennel and let them cool. Slice each sausage on the diagonal into thirds.

Alternately thread pieces of sausage, fennel, and mushroom onto 8 skewers. Transfer the skewers to a sealable container just large enough to hold them and refrigerate until you are ready to pack, up to 8 hours.

At the tailgate Prepare coals for a medium fire. When the coals are ready, brush the kabobs with the olive oil and sprinkle with the vinegar.

Grill the kabobs, turning once, until the sausages are lightly browned, about 6 minutes. Serve hot.

★ ★ ★

SEA SCALLOP AND BACON KABOBS

Serves 4

Sea scallops are the bigger ones, which can stand up to the grill. Still they need to be cooked for only a short time. Turn your head for a moment and they'll be done. Kind of like what would happen to a lineman when Barry Sanders was carrying the ball—turn your head for a moment and *you* were done.

- **8 ounces sliced bacon**
- **2 pounds sea scallops**
- **3 small zucchini, cut in half lengthwise, then into 1-inch pieces**
- **3 tablespoons olive oil**
- **3 tablespoons fresh lemon juice**
- **4 cloves garlic, finely chopped**
- **¼ cup finely chopped fresh basil or parsley**
- **1 teaspoon salt**
- **1 teaspoon ground black pepper**
- **1 lemon, cut into quarters**

At home Pour an inch of water into a skillet and bring to a boil over high heat. Add the bacon strips and, when the water returns to a boil, reduce the heat to low and simmer for 2 minutes. Transfer the bacon to paper towels and pat dry. Cut the strips roughly in half crosswise.

Wrap each scallop in a slice of bacon. Alternately thread the wrapped scallops with the zucchini pieces onto 8 skewers. Transfer to a sealable container just large enough to hold them and refrigerate until ready to pack, up to 2 hours.

In a small, sealable container, mix together the olive oil, lemon juice, garlic, basil, salt, and pepper. Refrigerate until you are ready to pack, up to 2 hours.

At the tailgate Prepare coals for a medium-hot fire.

While the coals are heating, brush the kabobs with the olive oil mixture.

When the coals are ready, grill the kabobs for 5 to 6 minutes, turning them a quarter turn every minute or so, until they are almost completely opaque in the center (they will finish cooking off the heat).

Serve immediately, with lemon juice squeezed over them.

Put Me In, Coach! Ready-to-Serve Entrées

These dishes are ready to play. They are served at room temperature, and they are completely done. No grill. No burner. No last-minute nothing. Maybe they're not as jazzy as some of the other dishes. On the other hand, they are convenient and flavorful. If you are joining up with another tailgate party and they are doing the grill, you can bring along one of these dishes as another main course.

Note:

These dishes are designed to be cooked entirely at home.

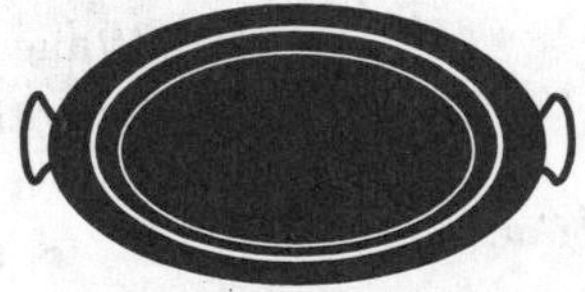

Tailgating Tales

DON'T MESS WITH TEXAS BRISKET

Fred Olds has not missed a regularly scheduled Texas A&M Aggies home football game in 31 years. The one game he did miss was in 1978. Because of a hurricane, a Saturday game had to be rescheduled to a Thursday. This conflicted with work. Barely, but enough. And the streak was broken. As a result of his dedication, Fred is one of the *eminences grises* of Aggie tailgating. Over the years his location has improved, and now his RV is parked directly next to the stadium. Food, though, is secondary to football when the Oldses tailgate. What does come first is family and friends. Fred does have one tried-and-true recipe, which, through his three decades of tailgating, he has honed and refined to a state of near perfection. Here it is: "Take a six-pack of beer, put it in the fridge, and wait two hours. Then serve." If you wish to say hello to Fred and Jean Olds, you'll find them next to the legendary Church Bus, so named because the two Aggie fans who bought it at auction left the name of the previous owner, a church, on the side. The church might not have minded had not holes been drilled through the side wall of the bus and two spigots placed there, from which cold beer flows for all who want. (A collection box sits next to the spigots.) The church's name has since been painted over, but the bus is still there. Fred usually packs sandwiches for his tailgating, but he's not averse to wandering around the parking lot visiting old friends and freeloading on the Texas barbecued brisket that is so prevalent among Aggie fans.

★ ★ ★

OVEN-BARBECUED BRISKET

Serves 8

Not genuine, authentic Texas smoked brisket, but man is this meat good. I think even Fred Olds would approve.

- **2 large onions, cut in half lengthwise and thinly sliced**
- **5 pounds first-cut beef brisket**
- **1 cup beef broth**
- **2 tablespoons liquid smoke**
- **½ cup ketchup**
- **¼ cup Worcestershire sauce**
- **2 tablespoons brown sugar**
- **6 cloves garlic, coarsely chopped**
- **4 canned chipotle chiles in adobo sauce, coarsely chopped**
- **3 tablespoons chili powder**
- **White bread for serving**
- **1 cup Homemade Barbecue Sauce (page 168)**

At home Preheat the oven to 325°F. Lay the onion slices on the bottom of a roasting pan just large enough to hold the brisket. Lay the brisket on top of the onions.

In a medium bowl, stir together the beef broth, liquid smoke, ketchup, Worcestershire sauce, brown sugar, garlic, chipotle chiles, and chili powder until combined, and pour over the brisket.

Cover the pan tightly with a double layer of aluminum foil. Cook on the middle rack of the oven for 2 hours and 45 minutes.

Remove the brisket from the oven, put the pan in a brown paper grocery bag, close it up, and let the brisket sit for another hour.

Transfer the brisket to a cutting board and slice it against the grain and on the diagonal into ¼-inch slices. Skim the fat from the gravy and return the slices to the pan. Transfer to a sealable container.

At the tailgate Serve the brisket warm or at room temperature on slices of white bread, with some barbecue sauce.

★ ★ ★

ORZO WITH ARTICHOKES AND SHRIMP

Serves 6

The problem with most pasta salads is that there's too much pasta and not enough stuff. This one has more stuff.

PESTO

- **4** cups fresh basil leaves, washed and dried
- **2** cloves garlic
- **3** tablespoons pine nuts
- **½** teaspoon salt
- **¼** cup plus 2 tablespoons olive oil
- **¼** cup grated Parmesan cheese

- **12** ounces orzo
- **6** tablespoons olive oil
- **2** pounds large shrimp, shelled and deveined
- **6** cloves garlic, finely chopped
- Salt and ground black pepper
- **1** medium red onion, finely chopped
- **2** cans (16 ounces each) artichoke hearts, drained and each choke cut in quarters
- **1** jar (12 ounces) roasted red peppers, drained and diced
- **8** ounces cherry tomatoes, cut in half lengthwise
- **2** ounces kalamata olives, pitted and chopped

At home **For the pesto:** Put the basil, garlic, pine nuts, salt, olive oil, and Parmesan in the bowl of a food processor fitted with the metal blade. Process until the mixture just becomes a smooth paste. You'll need ¾ cup of the pesto for the salad. Store in the refrigerator in a covered container with a layer of plastic wrap pressed on the surface of the pesto. It lasts for 1 week in the refrigerator or 2 months in the freezer.

Cook the orzo in a large pot of salted boiling water. When it is al dente, drain and rinse briefly with cold water to stop the cooking. Transfer to a large bowl and toss with 2 tablespoons of the olive oil.

Place a large skillet over high heat and let it get very hot, about 2 minutes. Add 2 tablespoons of the olive oil and spread it evenly over the pan. Add half the shrimp and cook until they are almost cooked through, about five minutes. Add half the garlic, season with salt and pepper and cook for 1 minute more, stirring continuously. Transfer the cooked shrimp to the bowl with the orzo. Return the pan to the heat, add the 2 tablespoons remaining olive oil, and repeat with the remaining shrimp and garlic.

Add the onion, artichoke hearts, red peppers, tomatoes, olives, ¾ cup pesto, and salt and pepper to taste. Mix everything together so the orzo is coated with the pesto. Correct the seasoning if necessary, transfer to a sealable container, and refrigerate for up to 4 hours.

At the tailgate Allow the salad to return to room temperature before serving.

★ ★ ★

THE BIG SANDWICH

Serves 6

The Big Sandwich is easy and fun to make and usually satisfies your friends who are thinking more about throwing the football around the parking lot than they are about the food. The Big Sandwich started out as an attempt to make the New Orleans classic loaf-size sandwich–the muffaletta. It has evolved over the years, with my friend Mark's inspired introduction of the anchovies. You can concoct pretty much any collage of meats and cheeses you want, though I always use proportionally less hard salami, which tends to overwhelm the other flavors.

- **1 cup coarsely chopped pitted green olives**
- **¼ cup coarsely chopped pepperoncini**
- **4 anchovy fillets, coarsely chopped**
- **¼ cup Italian dressing**
- **¼ cup olive oil**
- **1 round loaf Italian or French bread, cut through the middle**
- **4 ounces mortadella, thinly sliced**
- **4 ounces hot capicola, thinly sliced**
- **4 ounces turkey breast, thinly sliced**
- **2 ounces sopressata or other hard salami, thinly sliced**
- **2 ounces mozzarella cheese, thinly sliced**
- **1 jar (4 ounces) roasted red peppers, drained and cut into strips**
- **2 cups shredded lettuce**

At home In a small bowl, mix together the olives, pepperoncini, anchovies, Italian dressing, and olive oil and, if possible, refrigerate overnight.

Lay a double-wide 18-inch length of plastic wrap on a work surface. Scoop out about half of the inside of both sides of the loaf of bread. Place the bottom half of the bread in the center of the plastic wrap.

Spoon half of the olive mixture over the bottom half of the bread. Arrange layers of the mortadella, capicola, turkey, sopressata, and mozzarella over the olive mixture, going all the way to the edge of the bread. Arrange the pepper strips over the cheese, then add the lettuce. Top with the remaining olive mixture and the top half of the bread.

Wrap the Big Sandwich, not too tightly, in the plastic and set it on a large plate. Set another plate or a cast-iron skillet on top of the sandwich and weigh it down with some cans or a (full) six-pack. Refrigerate for 1 hour and up to 4 hours.

At the tailgate Unwrap the sandwich, cut into 6 wedges, and serve.

Tailgating Tales

HOAGIE HEROS

Mike Friedman has been a Philadelphia Eagles fan his whole life. He's been tailgating long enough to remember when they began discussing plans to build the new Veterans Stadium. Politicians, city fathers, and regular football fans all weighed in about the financing, the architecture, the sight lines at the new Vet. There was much heated discussion about better seating and more corporate boxes. But that was all incidental to Mike. Like any serious tailgater, his first concern was the parking lot. Was it going to be bigger? Smaller? Have more tailgating sites? More portable toilets? Fortunately for Mike and his tailgating comrades, the new Vet went up on the other side of the parking lot from the old Vet. So in a sense, the tailgaters got to stay where they were, just needing to reorient the direction of their tents (which for some actually caused a fair amount of confusion). Then, once the new Vet opened, came the Hoagie War. Under the guise of searching for weaponry after 9/11, the Eagles front office instituted a ban on bringing any food into Veterans Stadium. Fans who'd packed their hoagies had to eat them at the gate or toss them out. Coincidentally, there was plenty of food for sale inside the stadium. Food some patrons felt was prohibitively expensive. And not so good. They thought about the hoagies they had abandoned at the gate. They weren't happy. A publicity war ensued, waged on the front pages of the sports section, and soon the stadium brass relented, though the hoagies had to be carried in clear plastic bags, their hoagie-ness clearly visible. The fans had won.

THE HOAGIE

Serves 4

The bread is what makes the hoagie. They are sometimes called Atlantic City rolls or Amaroso rolls, but you will know them because they are crusty (but not artisanal bread crusty) outside and soft and doughy inside. This bread may not be authentic enough to grace the table at a fine Italian restaurant (one with cloth as opposed to vinyl tablecloths), but it's the right bread for a hoagie.

4 crusty-outside-but-soft-inside sub rolls
¼ cup Italian dressing
¼ cup mayonnaise
8 ounces ham, thinly sliced
8 ounces salami, thinly sliced
8 ounces provolone cheese, thinly sliced
½ cup hot pepperoncini slices
½ cup sweet pepper slices
2 cups shredded lettuce
1 medium red onion, thinly sliced
2 tablespoons dried oregano

At home Cut the bread in half lengthwise but not all the way through. Spoon some of the Italian dressing on the top of the bread and spread some of the mayonnaise on the bottom. Fill the bread with slices of the ham, salami, and cheese. Add some of the pepperoncini, sweet peppers, lettuce, and onion. Sprinkle with the oregano and wrap in plastic wrap and then in aluminum foil.

Note Try to make your hoagies close enough to game time that you don't have to refrigerate them. The cold messes up the consistency of the bread, and the sandwich loses its zeitgeist.

★ ★ ★

FRIED CHICKEN

Serves 4

You'll find fried chicken wherever there is tailgating. It can be prepared any number of ways, all of which are absolutely authentic and the best fried chicken ever made—just ask the person who cooked it. Although this one is not my family's secret recipe handed down through the generations (fried chicken wasn't exactly ever a popular Russian dish, either before or after the Revolution), I can vouch for its excellence.

1 chicken (3 to 4 pounds), cut into 8 pieces
2 cups buttermilk
1 cup unbleached all-purpose flour
¾ teaspoon baking powder
Salt
½ teaspoon cayenne
2 cups peanut or vegetable oil
Ground black pepper

At home Arrange the chicken pieces in a casserole and pour the buttermilk over them. Refrigerate overnight.

Take the chicken out of the refrigerator a few hours before cooking and let it come to room temperature. Remove the chicken from the buttermilk and pat dry.

Place the flour, baking powder, 1 tablespoon of salt, and the cayenne in a heavy paper grocery bag. Fold the top of the bag and shake a few times to combine. Add the chicken pieces, fold the top of the bag, and shake a few times to coat the chicken.

In a large skillet, heat the peanut oil over high heat to 350°F. Add the chicken pieces gently, being careful not to splash the oil. Lower the heat to medium-high and cook for 10 minutes. Turn the chicken and cook until the juices run clear when the thigh meat is pierced, about 10 more minutes. Transfer to paper towels. Season with salt and pepper and let the chicken cool.

Note It's best to make fried chicken the morning of the game. When packing for the tailgate, do not store the chicken in a sealed container. This will turn it soggy. A cardboard box like they use at the fried chicken store works well. Otherwise, drape a clean kitchen towel over the container and secure it with a rubber band so the chicken can breathe.

★ ★ ★

ROTISSERIE CHICKEN SALAD

Serves 6

If George Steinbrenner can buy himself a pennant, you can buy a cooked chicken. Strip the meat off the bone with your hands and you've pretty much got this one done.

2 cooked deli or rotisserie chickens
2 cups chopped celery or fennel or a combination
1 medium red onion, finely chopped
4 ounces oil-packed sun-dried tomatoes, coarsely chopped
½ cup coarsely chopped fresh basil
¼ cup mayonnaise
¼ cup sour cream
1 teaspoon salt
1 teaspoon ground black pepper

At home Remove the meat from the chicken, checking carefully that you did not get any bits of bone or cartilage. Chop or tear the chicken roughly into 1½- to 2-inch pieces and put them in a large bowl. Add the celery, onion, sun-dried tomatoes, and basil.

In a small bowl, stir together the mayonnaise, sour cream, salt, and pepper. Add the dressing to the bowl with the chicken and mix together until the dressing is evenly distributed. Transfer to a sealable container and refrigerate until ready to pack, up to 4 hours.

At the tailgate Serve at room temperature.

PULLED PORK SANDWICHES

Serves 8 to 10

You will need to spend most of the afternoon the day before the game preparing this. You're going to have to take my word for it that it's worth the effort. It's the real deal. An aluminum pan of chopped barbecue is like a suitcase of unmarked hundreds. Or an envelope with a pair of Packer tickets. Just heat up the chopped pork, dish it out between the attendant slices of white bread, and you will have a spread that will be the envy of a parking lot filled with even the most ardent brat lovers.

3 tablespoons sweet paprika
2 tablespoons chili powder
2 tablespoons ground cumin
2 tablespoons brown sugar
2 tablespoons kosher salt
1 tablespoon ground black pepper
1 tablespoon granulated sugar
1 bone-in Boston butt or pork shoulder (6 to 8 pounds)
2 cups hickory or other hardwood chips
3 cups Homemade Barbecue Sauce (page 168)
20 slices white bread

At home In a small bowl, mix together the paprika, chili powder, cumin, brown sugar, salt, pepper, and granulated sugar until well combined.

Cut away any skin from the pork (you can ask the butcher to do this if you want, but it's not hard.) Rub the entire roast with the spices, wrap it in plastic, and refrigerate for at least 12 hours and up to 24 hours.

Two hours before cooking, soak the wood chips in water to cover.

Prepare coals for a medium fire. While the coals are heating, unwrap the pork and place it in an aluminum pan just big enough to hold it.

Lay a 12-inch, double layer of aluminum foil on a work surface. Place half the wood chips in the center, then fold to make a neat package. Poke 6 holes in the top to release the smoke during cooking. Repeat with the remaining wood chips.

When the coals are ready, distribute them on opposite sides of the grill and open the bottom vents. Place one of the packages of wood chips on one of the piles of coals and set the grill rack in place. Set the pan of pork in the center of the rack and open the top vents. Smoke the pork for 3 hours, adding a handful of coals every 40 minutes or so. Halfway through cooking, place the second package of wood chips on the coals.

Twenty minutes before you finish smoking, preheat the oven to 325°F.

Remove the pan of pork from the grill, cover it tightly with aluminum foil, and transfer it to the oven. Cook on the center rack until the meat is tender, about 2 hours.

Open 4 sheets of newspaper (preferably the sports section) on a work surface. Remove the pan of pork from the oven and place it in the center of the newspaper. Wrap the pan in the newspaper as you would a precious gift, and let it sit for 1 hour.

Remove the newspaper and aluminum foil and transfer the pork to a cutting board. When cool enough to handle, separate the large pieces of meat from the bone and shred them with your fingers. In a medium bowl, toss the shredded pork with 1 cup of the barbecue sauce, adding more to taste, but not too much, as people will add more later when they make their sandwiches. Transfer the pork to a medium pot, place on the stove top, and heat over medium heat, stirring continuously, until it is quite hot. Wrap the pot in several layers of newspaper and pack it in a Styrofoam cooler. It should stay hot for an hour or so and will keep warm for about 2 hours.

At the tailgate Place a heaping portion of the pork on one slice of bread. Top with more barbecue sauce and the other slice of bread, take a deep breath, and eat heartily.

Homemade Barbecue Sauce

Makes 3 cups

This is a rich, complex sauce worthy of the time and effort you put into making your pulled pork. After all, you don't put a Picasso in a Dollar Store frame.

- **1 medium onion, finely chopped**
- **6 cloves garlic, finely chopped**
- **2 cups ketchup**
- **¾ cup fresh orange juice**
- **¼ cup water**
- **¼ cup fresh lemon juice**
- **2 tablespoons red wine vinegar**
- **2 tablespoons tomato paste**
- **2 tablespoons honey**
- **2 tablespoons brown sugar**
- **2 tablespoons molasses**
- **2 tablespoons Worcestershire sauce**
- **2 tablespoons Dijon mustard**
- **1 tablespoon chili powder**
- **1 teaspoon liquid smoke**
- **1 teaspoon ground coriander**
- **1 teaspoon Tabasco or other hot sauce**

At home In a heavy-bottomed saucepan, mix all the ingredients together and bring to a boil over medium heat. Reduce the heat to low and simmer for 10 minutes, stirring frequently.

Let cool and refrigerate for up to 1 week.

16
SF

★★★

CAJUN MEAT LOAF SANDWICHES

Serves 6

When you want to serve meat and you don't feel like dealing with the grill, this is the way to go. I like my meat loaf sandwiches on pumpernickel bread with classic Heinz chili sauce and a few shots of hot sauce. You can also pile on some coleslaw; no one would mind.

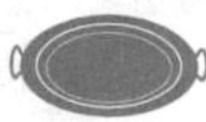

16 slices white bread, 4 torn into 1-inch pieces
½ cup milk
2 tablespoons olive oil
1 medium onion, finely chopped
1 red bell pepper, cored, seeded, and finely chopped
8 scallions, green parts only, finely chopped
4 cloves garlic, finely chopped
1 tablespoon chili powder
1 tablespoon Cajun seasoning
1 teaspoon cayenne
1 pound ground beef
8 ounces ground pork
2 andouille sausages (4 ounces total), cut into ½-inch pieces
½ cup chili sauce
1 egg
1 teaspoon hot sauce
Lettuce and sliced red onion for serving
Chili sauce for serving

At home Preheat the oven to 350°F. In a small bowl, mix together the torn bread and milk and set aside.

Heat the olive oil in a large skillet over medium-high heat. Add the onion, bell pepper, and scallions and cook over low heat until soft, about 8 minutes. Add the garlic and cook for 1 minute more. Add the chili powder, Cajun seasoning, and cayenne and cook for 1 minute more, stirring continuously. Remove the vegetables from the heat and transfer to a large mixing bowl. Let the mixture cool slightly.

Add the beef, pork, sausages, soaked bread pieces, chili sauce, egg, and hot sauce to the vegetables and mix with your hands until well combined. Transfer to a 9-by-5-inch loaf pan and pat down gently.

Bake on the center rack of the oven for 1 hour. Let cool, wrap in aluminum foil, and refrigerate for up to 24 hours.

At the tailgate Let the meat loaf come to room temperature. Cut it into 1½-inch slices. Arrange on a slice of bread, top with lettuce, onion, some chili sauce, and a second slice of bread.

Note If you have your grill going for something else and you want to serve the meat loaf hot, grill the slices for about 1 minute on each side, until they are heated through.

SI

ES

You don't need an abundance of sides at a tailgate, but you do need some. They make the party more complete. Not just in terms of the food, but the whole spirit of the event. Your side dishes subtly make the point that we're not here just to consume what comes off the grill. We've gathered to be together, not just to wolf down a steak, but to have a meal. To mingle and tell stories. Seeing the table spread with platters filled with more than just meat encourages this kind of interaction. It doesn't mean you can't try to eat more pulled pork sandwiches than any human being should, but you will at least have a conversation while you are doing it.

Reheating sides at a tailgate can sometimes be a hassle. Capacious tailgaters, those towing a trailer packed with enough hardware to launch a small invasion, have chafing dishes specifically designated for all their side dishes. Other equally dedicated tailgaters do what they can, but in general they don't treat the presentation of their side dishes so preciously. They know that the potato salad doesn't have to be refrigerator cold and the red beans and rice don't need to be hotter than room temperature, especially if you're tailgating on the infield at Daytona, where it can get as hot as an oven anyway.

RED BEANS AND RICE

Serves 8

You can't go wrong with red beans and rice. It goes with barbecue, burgers, and any main course that has a hint of Mexican flavor.

3 tablespoons olive oil
1 cup finely chopped onion
4 ounces andouille or other smoked, spicy sausage, cut into ½-inch pieces
6 cloves garlic, finely chopped
1½ cups white rice
1 can (4 ounces) diced green chiles, drained
¼ cup purchased salsa
1 cup tomato sauce, preferably spicy Mexican style
1 can (12 ounces) red or black beans, drained
2½ cups chicken broth
1 teaspoon dried oregano
1 teaspoon salt

At home Place a medium skillet over medium-high heat and let it get hot, about 2 minutes. Add 2 tablespoons of the olive oil and spread it evenly over the pan. Add the onion and cook, stirring occasionally, until it begins to soften, about 6 minutes. Add the sausage and garlic and cook for 2 minutes more.

Add the remaining tablespoon olive oil and the rice and stir so all the rice is coated lightly with oil, about 2 minutes.

Add the chiles, salsa, tomato sauce, beans, chicken broth, oregano, and salt and stir to combine. Bring the mixture to a boil, then immediately reduce the heat to low, cover, and cook until the rice is just cooked through, about 18 minutes.

Let cool and transfer to a sealable container. Refrigerate, covered, for up to 24 hours.

At the tailgate Bring the beans and rice to room temperature before serving, or reheat, adding ½ cup water, broth, or tomato sauce to keep the dish moist. Stir continuously while reheating to keep the rice from scorching.

CORN AND BLACK BEAN SALAD

Serves 6

This salad is a natural for Steeler fans keen on tailgating with food in the predominantly yellow and black motif.

- **1 can (14 ounces) black beans, drained**
- **2 cans (8 ounces each) corn kernels packed in water, drained**
- **1 medium red onion, finely chopped**
- **2 green bell peppers, cored, seeded, and finely chopped**
- **1 red bell pepper, cored, seeded, and cut into quarters**
- **1 jalapeño chile, stemmed, seeded, and finely chopped**
- **½ cup finely chopped fresh cilantro**
- **¼ cup olive oil**
- **2 tablespoons fresh lime juice**
- **½ teaspoon chili powder**
- **½ teaspoon ground cumin**
- **1 teaspoon salt**

At home In a medium bowl, mix together the beans, corn, onion, green and red bell peppers, jalapeño, and cilantro.

In a small bowl, whisk together the olive oil, lime juice, chili powder, cumin, and salt. Pour the dressing over the corn and bean mixture and stir together. Transfer to a sealable container and refrigerate for up to 6 hours.

At the tailgate Bring the salad to room temperature before serving.

★ ★ ★

GRILLED CORN

Serves 6

Great quarterbacks find a way to get the ball to a receiver even when there seems to be no apparent opening, eliciting from the announcer the reverential refrain, "How did he get that ball in there?" One of the skills of a great tailgate grill man is finding a way to get the ears of corn on the grill under similar conditions. He'll nudge and reposition the meat, using every inch of the grill to fit the corn on. He knows how much everyone is waiting for it, how grilling transforms the corn, bringing out its sweetness. He knows how much the tailgate team is depending on his arm.

6 ears of corn
Butter for serving
Salt for serving

At the tailgate Prepare coals for a medium-hot fire. While the coals are heating, remove all but the last layer of husk from each ear of corn. (The kernels should be covered but just visible through the last layer.) When the coals are ready, grill the corn until it darkens, 8 to 10 minutes, turning it every 2 minutes or so to cook it evenly. Serve with the salt and butter.

Note Grilled corn is also great even if it's not fresh off the fire. If you're cooking for a big crowd, fill the grill with corn first and cook it. You can then let it sit, covered with a clean kitchen cloth, while you grill the main course.

COUSCOUS SALAD

Serves 6

Couscous is often overlooked as a side, but it cooks in minutes and its Middle Eastern flavor goes with lamb, ham, the Curried Beef Kabobs (page 145), smoked salmon, or a grilled steak.

- **2 cups water**
- **2 teaspoons salt, plus more as needed**
- **1 cup (about 6 ounces) couscous**
- **1 cup finely chopped celery**
- **1 medium red onion, finely chopped**
- **4 scallions, green parts only, finely chopped**
- **1 cup dried cranberries or currants**
- **1 cup cooked chickpeas**
- **3 tablespoons ground ginger**
- **2 tablespoons ground cinnamon**
- **1 tablespoon ground cumin**
- **½ cup extra-virgin olive oil**
- **Ground black pepper**

At home Bring the water and 2 teaspoons salt to a boil in a medium saucepan. Add the couscous and stir once. As soon as the water returns to a boil, remove the saucepan from the heat, cover it, and let it rest for 5 minutes. Transfer the couscous to a sheet pan and spread it out to cool for 10 minutes.

Transfer the couscous to a medium bowl with your hands, breaking up any clumps with your fingers. Add the celery, onion, scallions, cranberries, chickpeas, ginger, cinnamon, cumin, olive oil, and pepper to taste. Toss together until combined. Add more salt if necessary. Transfer to a sealable container and refrigerate, covered, for up to 2 hours.

At the tailgate Let the salad come to room temperature before serving.

Note The consistency and flavor of this salad do not improve in the refrigerator, so try to prepare it as close to your party time as possible.

★ ★ ★

MEDITERRANEAN-STYLE POTATO SALAD

Serves 6

An alternative to the mayonnaise-based classic, this potato salad features lots of fresh basil and olive oil.

- **3 pounds small red potatoes, cut in half**
- **1 small bulb fennel, cut into ½-inch dice**
- **1 jar (4 ounces) roasted red peppers, drained and coarsely chopped**
- **4 ounces oil-packed sun-dried tomatoes, drained, with oil reserved**
- **1 medium red onion, cut into ½-inch dice**
- **¼ cup chopped fresh parsley**
- **¼ cup chopped fresh basil, or 2 teaspoons dried basil**
- **About ¼ cup olive oil**
- **2 tablespoons red wine vinegar**
- **1 teaspoon Dijon mustard**
- **Salt and ground black pepper**

At home In a large saucepan, bring the potatoes to a boil in enough cold water to cover them by an inch. Reduce the heat to low and simmer until the potatoes are just cooked through, 16 to 18 minutes. (Remember, they'll continue cooking a bit longer after you remove them from the pot.) Drain well in a colander, transfer to a large sealable container, and let cool for about 20 minutes, gently turning the potatoes with a rubber spatula to allow the bottom ones to cool as well.

Add the fennel, red peppers, sun-dried tomatoes, onion, parsley, and basil. Seal the container and refrigerate for up to 4 hours.

Combine the reserved oil from the tomatoes with enough olive oil to make ¼ cup. In a small, sealable container, whisk together the oil, vinegar, mustard, and salt and pepper to taste.

At the tailgate Pour the dressing over the potato mixture, gently toss together, and serve.

TAILGATING TALES

BREWERMANIA

Craig Bauhmann comes from a family of serious Milwaukee baseball fans. His grandfather got season tickets to the Brewers the day they moved to Milwaukee from Boston. They have been in the family ever since. Craig sold beer in old Milwaukee County Stadium to help pay for college, and he now tailgates in Miller Field before at least a dozen Brewers games a season. He has a favorite spot in the parking lot, chosen (as many in-the-know tailgaters do) for being not too close but not too far away from a bank of portable toilets. He doesn't stray far from traditional Wisconsin fare, and gets his brats from House of Homemade Sausage in Germantown. If it's particularly crowded and the traffic is moving slowly out of the lot, Craig will often indulge in a postgame tailgate meal. He has a special menu saved for just such an occasion—grilled brats, also known, affectionately, as "more of the same."

★ ★ ★

CRAIG'S POTATO PACKETS

Serves 4

Here's an easy way to have hot potatoes without much effort. They need 14 minutes of time on the grill, which means starting them a few minutes before you cook your brats or burgers.

2 pounds Yukon Gold potatoes, thinly sliced
1 red bell pepper, cored, seeded, and thinly sliced
1 medium onion, cut in half lengthwise and thinly sliced
2 cloves garlic, finely chopped
2 tablespoons olive oil
Salt and ground black pepper

At home Lay two 16-inch lengths of aluminum foil on a work surface.

Put the potatoes, bell pepper, onion, and garlic in a large bowl. Pour the olive oil over them, sprinkle with salt and pepper, and toss together until combined.

Arrange half the potato mixture in the center of each piece of aluminum foil. Bring the long ends together and fold them tightly several times. Then fold up the sides to make a neat, sealed packet.

At the tailgate Prepare coals for a medium-hot fire. When the coals are ready, place the potato packets on the rack and cook for 7 minutes. Turn and cook for 7 minutes more.

Open the packets carefully to avoid the escaping steam and serve. Each packet serves 2.

COCONUT RICE WITH MANGOES AND BLACK BEANS

Serves 6

This quick rice goes well with any of the Asian and Caribbean dishes.

- **1 can (15 ounces) unsweetened coconut milk**
- **½ medium onion, sliced**
- **1 clove garlic**
- **6 sprigs cilantro, plus ¼ cup coarsely chopped fresh cilantro**
- **2 scallions, both white and green parts, cut into 1-inch pieces**
- **½ teaspoon ground ginger**
- **1 teaspoon salt**
- **1½ cups chicken broth**
- **1½ cups rice**
- **2 mangoes, peeled, pitted, and cut into ½-inch pieces**
- **1 can (14 ounces) black beans, drained**

At home Put the coconut milk, onion, garlic, cilantro sprigs, scallions, ginger, and salt in a blender and purée until just smooth. Transfer to a medium saucepan and add the chicken broth and rice. Cover the pan and bring the liquid to a boil over medium heat. Reduce the heat to low and simmer until the rice is just cooked through, about 15 minutes.

Transfer the rice to a medium bowl. Add the mangoes, beans, and chopped cilantro and stir until just combined. Transfer to a sealable container and refrigerate for up to 4 hours.

At the tailgate Let the rice come to room temperature before serving.

★★★

WILD RICE SALAD WITH DRIED CRANBERRIES

Serves 6

A refreshing side that's great with meats, chicken, or fish. The nutty flavor of the wild rice is complemented by the sweetness of the cranberries.

- **3 cups water**
- **1½ cups wild rice**
- **1½ teaspoons salt**
- **1 cup dried cranberries**
- **1 red bell pepper, cored, seeded, and cut into ¼-inch dice**
- **1 yellow bell pepper, cored, seeded, and cut into ¼-inch dice**
- **2 carrots, peeled and grated**
- **6 scallions, green parts only, finely chopped**
- **¼ cup chopped fresh parsley**
- **¼ cup chopped fresh mint**
- **¼ cup fresh orange juice**
- **2 tablespoons fresh lemon juice**
- **1 tablespoon grated orange zest**
- **1 teaspoon Dijon mustard**
- **½ teaspoon salt, plus more as needed**
- **½ teaspoon ground black pepper**
- **¼ cup olive oil**

At home In a medium pot, combine the water, rice, and 1 teaspoon of the salt and bring to a boil. Immediately reduce the heat to low, cover, and simmer until the rice is cooked through but still has a bit of texture in the middle, about 50 minutes.

Drain the rice and transfer it to a sheet pan placed on a rack and spread it out to cool.

While the rice is cooling, soak the cranberries in very hot water to cover for 5 minutes. Drain and set aside.

When the rice is cool, transfer it to a large bowl and add the red and yellow bell peppers, carrots, scallions, parsley, mint, and the soaked cranberries and mix together.

In a small bowl, whisk together the orange juice, lemon juice, orange zest, mustard, ½ teaspoon salt, and pepper. Keep whisking and slowly pour in the olive oil.

Pour half of the dressing over the rice, mix together, and taste. Add more dressing and/or salt if needed. Refrigerate in a sealable container for up to 6 hours.

At the tailgate Let the salad come to room temperature and serve.

GRILLED RATATOUILLE

Serves 8

This is not your mother's ratatouille, assuming that she was even inclined to make it. The smoky, charred flavor of the grilled vegetables gives it a whole other dimension. If I happen to be grilling dinner for the family the night before a tailgate, I'll take advantage of the hot coals and cook the vegetables for the ratatouille. The flavor only improves with a stint in the fridge.

3 pounds eggplant (2 medium-large)
2 red bell peppers
2 pounds zucchini
1 large sweet onion
¼ cup Italian dressing
1 can (28 ounces) whole peeled tomatoes, juices reserved
3 tablespoons tomato paste
¼ cup chopped fresh basil, or 1 tablespoon dried basil
Salt and ground black pepper

At home Prepare a medium-hot fire in the grill.

While the coals are heating, trim the tops of the eggplant, peel, and cut them into ¾-inch rounds.

Trim the tops from the bell peppers and cut the peppers lengthwise into 4 sections. Trim away the white membrane.

Wash and dry the zucchini. Trim the tops and cut them lengthwise into ¾-inch strips.

Peel the onion, trim the ends, and cut crosswise into ½-inch rounds.

Arrange the vegetables on a platter and pour the dressing over them.

When the coals are ready, grill the eggplant slices until they are lightly browned, about 4 minutes. Turn and grill for about 4 minutes more.

Grill the zucchini until they are brown on each side, about 6 minutes, turning as needed to keep them from getting too charred.

Repeat with the bell peppers and onion.

Transfer the grilled vegetables to a cutting board. Cut the eggplant, zucchini, and bell peppers into 1-inch pieces. Cut the onion into coarse dice.

Transfer the chopped vegetables to a medium pot, add the tomatoes and their juice, tomato paste, basil, and salt and pepper to taste. Bring the mixture to a boil over high heat. Reduce the heat to low and simmer for 30 minutes. Let cool and transfer to a sealable container. Refrigerate for up to 2 days.

At the tailgate Reheat the ratatouille or serve it at room temperature.

Tailgating Tales

A TAILGATE BY ANY OTHER NAME

Chatham, Massachusetts, is home to the Chatham A's of the Cape Cod Summer League. Though situated in the heart of Red Sox country, Chatham A's fans have a charm and civility that are often absent from Fenway Park. When devoted fan Deborah Stewart packs up a lunch to tailgate before a Chatham A's game, she usually brings along some lobster rolls and a tub of her special coleslaw. She, along with other fans, prefer to say they "picnic" before the game in a nearby playground ("tailgating" being too evocative of blacktop for the idyll that is Cape Cod in summer) before heading to the park in time for the first pitch.

CAPE COD COLESLAW

Serves 8 to 10

It's always a good idea to have slaw when you're having barbecue. Not necessarily a lot, but a few forkfuls help to prepare the palate before you attack the next batch of ribs. The inclusion of the grated radish makes this version stand out among other slaws.

1 medium cabbage (about 2 pounds), cored and shredded
1 green bell pepper, cored, seeded, and thinly sliced
3 carrots, peeled and grated
1 medium red onion, thinly sliced
1 cup grated radish (about 4 ounces)
½ cup sour cream
¼ cup mayonnaise
1½ tablespoons cider vinegar
1 tablespoon Dijon mustard
1 tablespoon sugar
Salt and ground black pepper

At home In a large bowl, mix together the cabbage, bell pepper, carrots, onion, and radish.

In a small bowl, combine the sour cream, mayonnaise, vinegar, mustard, sugar, and salt and pepper to taste. Pour the dressing over the cabbage mixture and toss to combine. (This is best done with your hands.)

Transfer to a sealable container and refrigerate until ready to pack.

At the tailgate Serve chilled or at room temperature.

★ ★ ★

GREEN BEANS WITH HORSERADISH SAUCE

Serves 4

Horseradish sauce transforms ordinary green beans into a dish with some punch and audacity, the kind of spirit coaches like to see from Special Teams players like this.

2 cloves garlic, finely chopped
2 tablespoons olive oil
2 tablespoons mayonnaise
2 tablespoons prepared white horseradish
½ teaspoon sugar
½ teaspoon salt
Pinch of ground nutmeg
1 pound green beans, trimmed

At home In a small bowl, stir together the garlic, olive oil, mayonnaise, horseradish, sugar, salt, and nutmeg.

Steam the green beans until they are cooked but still crunchy. Transfer to a medium bowl and pour the sauce over them. Let cool and transfer to a sealable container. Refrigerate until ready to pack.

At the tailgate Serve the green beans chilled or at room temperature.

★ ★ ★

TUSCAN VEGETABLE PACKETS

Serves 4

These vegetables are sort of like a pizza without the crust. They're perfect accompaniment to steaks or chops.

1 can (8 ounces) artichoke hearts, drained and cut into 1-inch pieces
3 medium zucchini, cut into ¼-inch rounds
4 cups (about 4 ounces) baby spinach leaves, washed
2 plum tomatoes, cut into ¼-inch slices
4 ounces button mushrooms, stems trimmed, cut into ¼-inch slices
4 cloves garlic, finely chopped
2 tablespoons olive oil
1 teaspoon salt
6 slices bacon, excess fat trimmed, cut into 2-inch pieces
¼ cup grated Parmesan cheese

At home In a medium bowl, gently toss together the artichoke hearts, zucchini, spinach, tomatoes, mushrooms, and garlic with the olive oil and salt.

Lay two 16-inch lengths of aluminum foil on a work surface.

Arrange 3 slices of bacon on the center of each piece of foil. Arrange half the vegetables over each set of bacon slices. Divide the Parmesan evenly over both mounds of vegetables.

Bring the long ends of the foil together and fold them tightly several times. Then fold up the sides to make a neat, sealed packet.

At the tailgate Prepare coals for a medium-hot fire. When the coals are ready, place the packets on the rack and cook for 14 minutes.

Open the packets carefully to avoid the escaping steam, and serve. Each packet makes 2 servings.

★ ★ ★

GRILLED ASPARAGUS

Serves 4

If you've already got the charcoal going, there's really no reason not to serve grilled asparagus. It requires little effort to prepare and less to cook. It also looks great on a platter, which will earn kudos from anyone passing by.

- **1½ pounds asparagus, trimmed**
- **2 tablespoons olive oil**
- **2 teaspoons salt**

At home or at the tailgate Prepare coals for a medium-hot fire.

While the coals are heating, arrange the asparagus spears on a platter, pour the olive oil over them, and sprinkle with the salt. Toss gently so the spears are lightly coated with oil.

When the coals are ready, grill the spears for 4 to 6 minutes, depending on their thickness. They will be slightly charred when they are done.

Serve hot or at room temperature.

COWBOY BEANS

Serves 6

You'll feel like you're out on the range when you're serving these. If you have an extra cast-iron pan, use it to heat up the beans on the grill, then serve them right in the pan for an authentic cowboy feel.

2 tablespoons vegetable oil
½ cup finely chopped onion
½ cup finely chopped poblano chile or green bell pepper
4 ounces Canadian bacon, chopped
2 tablespoons finely chopped garlic
1 teaspoon chili powder
2 cans (15 ounces each) pinto beans, drained
¼ cup ketchup
¼ cup strong coffee
2 tablespoons Worcestershire sauce
1 tablespoon dark brown sugar
Dash of liquid smoke

At home Place a skillet, preferably cast iron, over medium-high heat and let it get hot, about 1 minute. Add the vegetable oil and the onion and poblano chile and cook until they soften, about 6 minutes. Add the bacon, garlic, and chili powder and cook for 1 minute more, stirring often. Add the beans, ketchup, coffee, Worcestershire sauce, brown sugar, and liquid smoke, and stir to combine. When the mixture starts to boil, reduce the heat to low and cook, partially covered, until the mixture thickens, about 10 minutes. Transfer to a sealable container and refrigerate until you are ready to pack, up to 24 hours.

At the tailgate Reheat the beans, and serve hot.

Tailgating Tales

WHEN IN ATHENS

Bulldogs rule in Athens, Georgia, home of the University of Georgia and its fabled football team. Lana Evans gets together with friends and family to tailgate every home game and root the Bulldogs to victory. Their meal usually centers around fried chicken and smoked ribs, the late afternoon kickoffs giving them enough time to get the ribs smoked without having to start the tailgating too early in the day. Everyone wears red, and visitors are encouraged to take part in the Bulldog Parade, which involves a tour of the painted bulldogs on display in front of many businesses in downtown Athens.

BULLDOG BROCCOLI SALAD

Serves 6

This salad is a great accompaniment to ribs and fried chicken, the two staples of Georgia Bulldog tailgating.

- **4 cups broccoli florets**
- **½ red bell pepper, cored, seeded, and cut into ½-inch dice**
- **1 medium red onion, finely chopped**
- **½ cup raisins**
- **½ cup slivered almonds**
- **2 tablespoons mayonnaise**
- **2 tablespoons sour cream**
- **1 tablespoon white wine vinegar or cider vinegar**
- **1 tablespoon sugar**
- **1 teaspoon mustard**
- **1 teaspoon salt**

At home Fill a large mixing bowl half full with cold water and dump in a tray of ice cubes. Bring a medium pot of water to a boil and blanch the broccoli florets for 1 minute. Remove them with a slotted spoon and plunge them into the bowl of ice water.

Drain the florets and pat them dry. Transfer to a large, sealable bowl and add the bell pepper, onion, raisins, and almonds.

In a small bowl, whisk together the mayonnaise, sour cream, vinegar, sugar, mustard, and salt. Transfer to a separate sealable container.

At the tailgate Pour the dressing over the broccoli mixture. Toss together, shout "Go Bulldogs!" and serve.

Tailgating Tales

FROM FOURTH AND LONG TO BEETHOVEN'S FOURTH

Annette Evans comes from a serious and dedicated tailgating family. And when she got married and moved near Interlochen, Michigan, home of the legendary summer music festival at the Interlochen School for the Arts, she figured hey, why not tailgate there? But since it's a classy locale, despite being surrounded by woods, she decided to do it up right. So for the past ten years, Annette's annual summer music tailgate party means tablecloths, linen napkins, candles, flowers, martinis in real glasses, and champagne with dinner. It's a far cry from the beer and brats she grew up with, but even kids who grew up on brats and beer like to have one night where they get to show a little class.

PAM'S ARTICHOKE RICE SALAD

Serves 4

This is one of the featured dishes at Annette's music tailgate parties.

- **1 box chicken Rice-a-Roni**
- **2 jars (6 ounces each) oil-packed artichoke hearts, drained, with oil reserved**
- **1 cup canned chickpeas, drained**
- **1 red bell pepper, cored, seeded, and finely chopped**
- **5 scallions, green parts only, finely chopped**
- **½ cup slivered almonds**
- **½ cup dried cranberries**
- **½ cup mayonnaise**
- **2 tablespoons fresh lemon juice**
- **1 tablespoon curry powder**
- **1 teaspoon salt**

At home Cook the Rice-a-Roni according to the package directions. When it is done, transfer it to a sheet pan and spread it out to cool.

Place the artichoke hearts, chickpeas, bell pepper, scallions, almonds, and cranberries in a large bowl. Add the cooled rice and toss together to combine.

In a small bowl, mix together the mayonnaise, reserved artichoke oil, lemon juice, curry powder, and salt. Pour the dressing over the rice mixture and fold to combine. Transfer to a sealable container and refrigerate for up to 12 hours.

At the tailgate Bring the salad to room temperature before serving.

★ ★ ★

SPICY CARROT SALAD

Serves 6

A little color, a little heat, and you have the perfect side dish for any entrée with an Asian kick.

¼ cup fresh lime juice (from about 2 large limes)
2 tablespoons olive oil
1 tablespoon Thai fish sauce
2 teaspoons sugar
2 teaspoons minced garlic
6 cups shredded carrots
1 jalapeño chile, stemmed, seeded, and finely chopped
½ cup roasted peanuts
1 teaspoon grated lime zest
Salt and ground black pepper

At home In a small bowl, mix together the lime juice, olive oil, fish sauce, sugar, and garlic.

In a large bowl, mix together the carrots, jalapeño, peanuts, and lime zest. Pour the dressing over the salad and toss to combine. Correct the seasoning if necessary, transfer to a sealable container and refrigerate until you are ready to pack, up to 24 hours.

At the tailgate Serve the salad chilled or at room temperature.

★ ★ ★

HAM AND CHEDDAR CHEESE BISCUITS

Makes 20 biscuits

Is it a biscuit? Is it a first course? Is it a meal because they're so tasty you can't resist eating too many? You decide.

- **4 cups unbleached all-purpose flour**
- **1 cup whole wheat flour**
- **¼ cup sugar**
- **2 tablespoons baking powder**
- **½ teaspoon cayenne**
- **2 teaspoons salt**
- **1 cup heavy cream**
- **1 cup buttermilk**
- **¾ cup (1½ sticks) butter, melted**
- **2 cups grated extra-sharp Cheddar cheese**
- **1 cup chopped smoked ham**

At home Preheat the oven to 350°F.

In a large bowl, whisk together the flours, sugar, baking powder, cayenne, and salt. In a separate bowl, stir together the cream, buttermilk, melted butter, cheese, and ham.

Add the wet ingredients to the dry and mix together with a wooden spoon until the dough pulls together but is still a little crumbly.

Turn the dough out onto a lightly floured work surface and knead gently until the dough is smooth, adding more flour if necessary.

Press the dough into an 8-by-16-inch rectangular shape about ¾ inch thick. Use a serrated knife to cut it into 20 squares. Transfer each square to an ungreased baking sheet, roughly re-creating the original shape, only with a ½-inch space between the biscuits.

Bake until the tops are lightly brown, about 35 minutes. Let the pan cool on a wire rack, then cover the pan with aluminum foil.

At the tailgate Arrange the biscuits in a cloth-lined basket or platter and serve.

★ ★ ★

FAKE-CACCIA

Serves 8

Not a real focaccia, which requires advanced baking skills, a proper oven, and flour harvested from the left side of the stalk by blindfolded virgins. This recipe doesn't need that kind of expertise. You should know, however, that of all the recipes for fake-caccia, this one is the most authentic.

1 tablespoon butter
¼ cup plus 1 tablespoon olive oil
2 medium onions, sliced about ¼ inch thick
1 jar (6 ounces) oil-packed artichoke hearts, drained and cut into ½-inch pieces
2 ounces oil-packed sun-dried tomatoes, cut into ¼-inch pieces
2 tablespoons brown sugar
2 cups unbleached all-purpose flour
1 tablespoon baking powder
1 teaspoon salt
1 teaspoon sugar
1 cup milk
1 egg
¼ cup olive oil
¼ cup grated Parmesan cheese

At home Preheat the oven to 350°F.

Place a medium skillet over medium-high heat, add the butter and 1 tablespoon of the olive oil, and let it get hot, about 2 minutes. Add the onions and cook, stirring occasionally, until they soften, about 10 minutes. Add the artichoke hearts and sun-dried tomatoes and cook for 2 minutes more. Remove from the heat and set aside.

Lightly grease a 9-inch square baking pan. Sprinkle the bottom with the brown sugar and arrange the onion mixture evenly over it.

In a large bowl, whisk together the flour, baking powder, salt, and sugar.

In a small bowl, combine the milk, egg, olive oil, and Parmesan. Add the wet ingredients to the dry and stir together until just combined. The dough will be a bit sticky—do not overmix.

Spread the dough over the onion mixture and bake until a toothpick inserted into the center comes out clean, 30 to 35 minutes. Let the pan cool on a wire rack, then cover the pan with aluminum foil to transport to the party.

At the tailgate Cut into rectangles, wrap in foil, and place on the coolest part of the grill for 4 to 5 minutes. You can sprinkle more Parmesan on top if you like.

★ ★ ★

GARLIC BREAD

Serves 6

Everyone likes garlic bread. It's basic. It's not flashy, but like a five-yard run off tackle on first down, even if it doesn't put points on the board, it makes everything else you run (or serve) that day easier and better.

1 loaf French or Italian bread

3 tablespoons butter

6 cloves garlic, finely chopped

1 teaspoon salt

At home Cut the bread lengthwise but not entirely through. Spread the butter and then the garlic on the bread. Sprinkle with the salt.

Cut the loaf in half crosswise and wrap each half in aluminum foil.

At the tailgate Prepare coals for a medium fire. When the coals are ready, heat the bread on the grill for 6 minutes, turning once. Unwrap, cut into slices, and serve.

★ ★ ★

SWEET AND SPICY CORN MUFFINS

Makes 12 muffins

It's expected that you'll have some kind of corn muffin around when you're making barbecue so people can soak up the sauce. These will take care of that responsibility, plus they'll fill in wherever else you need something sweet and spicy to serve with the meal.

- **1 cup unbleached all-purpose flour**
- **1 cup yellow cornmeal**
- **6 tablespoons sugar**
- **1 tablespoon baking powder**
- **1 teaspoon baking soda**
- **1½ teaspoons salt**
- **3 eggs**
- **1 cup sour cream**
- **½ cup (1 stick) butter, melted**
- **1 cup canned corn**
- **1 can (4 ounces) diced green chiles, drained**
- **1 jalapeño chile, stemmed, seeded, and finely chopped**

At home Preheat the oven to 350°F. Lightly grease a 12-cup muffin tin.

In a large bowl, whisk together the flour, cornmeal, sugar, baking powder, baking soda, and salt.

In a medium bowl, whisk together the eggs, sour cream, and melted butter. Stir in the corn, green chiles, and jalapeño.

Add the wet ingredients to the dry and stir until just combined. Do not over-mix. Fill each muffin cup three-fourths full of batter and bake on the center rack of the oven until a toothpick stuck into the center of a muffin comes out clean, 18 to 20 minutes.

Let the muffins cool in the tin on a wire rack, then run a small knife around the edge of each muffin before inverting the tin and liberating the muffins. Transfer to a sealable container and keep at room temperature until you are ready to pack, up to 8 hours.

At the tailgate The muffins will be ready to serve.

DESS

ERTS

Toward the end of a tailgate party, you may be feeling a kind of sensory overload. Between a cocktail or two, several courses of food, the marching band, some touch football, and a few group cheers, you may not feel as though you have room for anything else. But consider this—if you want to ensure that you are fostering the tailgating spirit in the next generation, you'd best have something special for dessert. Because that's what they'll remember. You'll lure a lot more kids to tailgating with brownies, chocolate cake, or Chocolate Pecan Pie than you will with box seats, even if they're on the 50-yard line. And to be honest, even though someone says they're too stuffed, that there's no possible way they could have even a morsel of dessert, as soon as you put it out they'll be hovering around, plate at the ready, shoving grandma out of the way to get the biggest piece.

★ ★ ★

CHOCOLATE PUDDING

Serves 8

Early one tailgating morning, I obtained 8 of those classic New York diner take-out coffee cups with the Greek-inspired design and filled them with this wonderful old-fashioned chocolate pudding. I kept the cups in the cooler, and just before we all headed into the stadium, I zapped them with some whipped cream and handed them out as a surprise treat. Everyone smiled.

- **1¼ cups sugar**
- **¼ cup unbleached all-purpose flour**
- **1 cup milk**
- **1 cup heavy cream**
- **8 ounces unsweetened chocolate**
- **½ teaspoon salt**
- **¼ teaspoon ground cinnamon**
- **1 egg**
- **1½ teaspoons vanilla extract**
- **½ cup (about 4 ounces) chopped pecans (optional)**
- **1 can pressurized whipped cream**

At home In a heavy saucepan, heat the sugar, flour, milk, cream, chocolate, salt, and cinnamon over medium-low heat. Stir continuously until the chocolate melts and the mixture comes to a boil. Immediately reduce the heat to low and continue cooking until the mixture thickens slightly, about 1 more minute. Remove from the heat.

In a medium bowl, whisk the egg until beaten. While you are whisking, slowly add ¼ cup of the chocolate mixture to the egg. When it is incorporated, slowly pour the egg mixture back into the saucepan, whisking continuously.

Return the saucepan to low heat and cook, stirring continuously, until the mixture thickens, about 2 minutes. Do not let the pudding boil or it will curdle.

Remove the pan from the heat and stir in the vanilla and the pecans, if desired.

Pour into 8 pudding cups or take-out coffee cups and refrigerate for at least 2 hours.

At the tailgate Serve the pudding topped with whipped cream.

★ ★ ★

PEACH AND BLUEBERRY "I FORGOT DESSERT" BREAD PUDDING

Serves 8

You use canned peaches and frozen blueberries for this bread pudding, allowing you to prepare it year-round, whenever you forget to make dessert.

- **3 eggs**
- **½ cup sugar**
- **1½ cups half-and-half**
- **2 teaspoons vanilla extract**
- **1 teaspoon finely chopped fresh ginger**
- **6 slices white bread, crusts trimmed, cut into 1-inch pieces**
- **1 bag (12 ounces) frozen blueberries**
- **1 can (14 ounces) peach halves, drained**
- **2 tablespoons butter**
- **2 tablespoons brown sugar**
- **1 can pressurized whipped cream**

At home Preheat the oven to 350°F. Butter a 9-inch square baking pan.

In a medium bowl, beat the eggs and sugar together until they lighten, about 4 minutes. Continue beating and slowly pour in the half-and-half. Add the vanilla and ginger.

Place the pieces of bread in a large bowl. Add the egg mixture and stir until just combined. Add the blueberries and stir until just combined, maybe 3 times.

Transfer the mixture to the prepared baking pan. Lay the peach halves on top, cut side down. Dot the top with the butter and sprinkle with the brown sugar.

Bake on the center rack of the oven until the pudding is just set, 35 to 40 minutes. It's better a little on the soft side.

This bread pudding is best made the morning of the party. Let it sit at room temperature for up to 8 hours. Cover with aluminum foil before transporting to the party.

At the tailgate Serve the bread pudding warm or at room temperature, with whipped cream.

★ ★ ★

CHOCOLATE CHUNK COOKIES

Makes 3 dozen cookies

A double wham of chocolate, a one-two punch like the great Packer running back combo of Taylor and Hornung. Keep these cookies hidden until the meal is done; otherwise all your hard work preparing the main course will be for naught.

12 ounces bittersweet chocolate
2½ cups unbleached all-purpose flour
¾ cup unsweetened cocoa powder
1 teaspoon baking soda
½ teaspoon salt
1 cup (2 sticks) butter, at room temperature
1 cup granulated sugar
1 cup packed brown sugar
2 eggs
1 tablespoon vanilla extract

At home Preheat the oven to 375°F.

Break the chocolate into ½-inch chunks and set aside.

In a small bowl, whisk together the flour, cocoa powder, baking soda, and salt.

In a large bowl, beat the butter with both sugars until smooth and creamy. Beat in the eggs, one at a time, until smooth. Stir in the vanilla and chocolate chunks.

Spoon about 1 tablespoon of dough for each cookie onto an ungreased cookie sheet, placing them about 1½ inches apart. Bake for 7 to 8 minutes.

Transfer the cookies to a wire rack and let cool to room temperature. Store in a sealable container until ready to serve.

OATMEAL RAISIN COOKIES

Makes 3 dozen cookies

Here's another way to keep the kids happy, along with some of the adults who may have reverted to childish behavior in their attempt to win the parking lot Wiffle ball game.

1¾ cups unbleached all-purpose flour
1 teaspoon baking soda
½ teaspoon ground cinnamon
Pinch of ground nutmeg
1 cup (2 sticks) butter, at room temperature
1 cup packed brown sugar
½ cup granulated sugar
2 large eggs
¼ cup milk
1 teaspoon vanilla extract
2½ cups rolled oats
1 cup raisins

At home Preheat the oven to 350°F.

In a medium bowl, whisk together the flour, baking soda, cinnamon, and nutmeg.

In a large bowl, beat the butter with both sugars until smooth and creamy. Beat in the eggs, one at a time, until smooth. Stir in the milk and vanilla. Add the oats, half at a time, and the raisins and stir to incorporate.

Spoon about 1 tablespoon of dough for each cookie onto an ungreased cookie sheet, placing them about 1½ inches apart. Bake for 10 minutes.

Transfer the cookies to a wire rack and let cool to room temperature. Store in a sealable container until ready to serve.

★ ★ ★

ALMOND BISCOTTI

Makes 2 ½ dozen biscotti

These crunchy cookies are perfect for dunking into a cup of coffee or hot chocolate before you head into the stadium. Stuff a few in your pocket to eat during the game.

- **2 cups unbleached all-purpose flour**
- **1 teaspoon baking powder**
- **½ teaspoon salt**
- **1 cup sugar**
- **2 large eggs**
- **½ teaspoon vanilla extract**
- **½ teaspoon almond extract**
- **½ cup almonds, coarsely chopped**

At home Preheat the oven to 350°F.

In a small bowl, whisk together the flour, baking powder, and salt.

In a large bowl, whisk together the sugar and eggs until they become a light yellow. Add the vanilla and almond extract and the chopped almonds.

Add the dry ingredients and stir together until just combined. Divide the dough in half and shape into two 13-by-2-inch logs. Lay each log on a lightly greased baking sheet and bake on the center rack of the oven until you see small cracks on the surface, about 35 minutes.

Remove and let cool for 10 minutes.

Lower the oven heat to 300°F. Use a serrated knife to cut the logs at an angle into ½-inch slices. Arrange the slices cut side up on the baking sheet and bake again for 15 minutes. Transfer the biscotti to a wire rack and let cool for 30 minutes. Pack in a sealable container until ready to serve.

★ ★ ★

KEY LIME PIE

Serves 8

You'll find these pies at tailgate parties all around Florida during football season and later in the spring when the Grapefruit League starts up.

¾ cup hazelnuts

4 ounces graham crackers, broken into pieces

½ cup plus 3 tablespoons sugar

6 tablespoons unsalted butter, melted

2 large eggs

1 can (14 ounces) sweetened condensed milk

⅓ cup fresh Key lime juice or regular lime juice (from 2 or 3 limes)

Pinch of salt

1 can pressurized whipped cream (optional)

At home Preheat the oven to 350°F.

Spread the hazelnuts on a baking sheet and roast in the oven until they brown slightly, about 10 minutes. Transfer to the bowl of a food processor fitted with a steel blade, along with the graham crackers, sugar, and melted butter. Process until well blended. (You can also do this in a bowl by first chopping the hazelnuts and graham crackers as finely as possible. Stir in the sugar and then the melted butter.)

Use your fingers to press the crust mixture onto the bottom and sides of a 9-inch pie plate.

Bake the crust on the center rack of the oven until it just begins to brown, about 8 minutes. Let it cool while you assemble the filling.

In a medium bowl, use an electric mixer to briefly beat the eggs, then add the condensed milk and beat well. With the mixer running, slowly pour in the lime juice, stopping at each third to incorporate. Beat in the salt.

Pour the mixture into the prepared crust and bake on the center rack until the pie is just firm in the middle, about 18 minutes.

Transfer the pie to a wire rack and let cool for at least an hour for the pie to fully set. Cover with plastic wrap and keep refrigerated until you are ready to pack, up to 24 hours.

At the tailgate Serve the pie topped with whipped cream, if desired.

CHOCOLATE PECAN PIE

Serves 8

A variation on a Southern tradition that's perfect after a meal of fried chicken or barbecue.

1 purchased frozen 9-inch pie shell
½ cup (1 stick) butter, melted
2 cups (about 8 ounces) pecan halves
¾ cup dark corn syrup
½ cup packed brown sugar
1 teaspoon vanilla extract
3 large eggs
8 ounces bittersweet chocolate, broken into ½-inch pieces, or jumbo chocolate chips

At home Preheat the oven to 425°F. Place a piece of foil over the pie shell and weigh it down with some dried beans, old fishing weights, ball bearings, or those washers you bought to fix the whatchamacallit in the basement, and bake on the center rack of the oven for 15 minutes. Remove the foil with the weights and bake the pie shell until the crust just starts turning a golden brown, about 5 minutes more. Transfer to a wire rack and let cool while you make the filling.

Coarsely chop half the pecans and set aside.

In a large bowl, whisk together the corn syrup, brown sugar, vanilla, and eggs until well mixed. Add the chopped and whole pecans and stir well. Pour the mixture into the pie shell. Sprinkle the chocolate pieces over the top, pressing them gently into the filling.

Bake on the center rack until the pie is set around the edge but still jiggles a bit in the center, 45 to 50 minutes.

Transfer the pie to a wire rack and let cool for at least an hour. Transfer to a sealable cake container and store at room temperature until you are ready to pack.

BROWNIES

Makes 16 brownies

Someone, somewhere, spread the word that baking brownies requires some kind of secret cabalistic knowledge of baking. That isn't true, as evidenced by this perfect brownie recipe.

8 ounces semisweet chocolate, broken into 1-inch pieces
½ cup (1 stick) butter, cut into 8 pieces
1 cup unbleached all-purpose flour
3 tablespoons unsweetened cocoa powder
½ teaspoon salt
3 large eggs
1 cup sugar
1 teaspoon vanilla extract

At home Preheat the oven to 350°F. Lightly butter an 8-inch square baking pan.

In a medium bowl placed over, but not touching, a pan with just simmering water, melt the chocolate and butter, stirring occasionally. When melted, set aside to cool slightly, about 5 minutes.

In a medium bowl, whisk together the flour, cocoa powder, and salt. Set aside.

In a separate bowl, whisk together the eggs, sugar, and vanilla. Add the chocolate and butter mixture and whisk until well combined. Add the dry ingredients and stir with a rubber spatula until just combined.

Transfer the batter to the prepared baking pan, spreading it into the corners of the pan. Bake on the center rack of the oven until a toothpick inserted into the center comes out flecked with crumbs (if it's smeared, it needs another few minutes), 30 to 35 minutes.

Let the brownies cool in the pan on a wire rack for 30 minutes before cutting them into 16 squares. Transfer to a sealable container and refrigerate until you are ready to pack, up to 24 hours.

At the tailgate The brownies will be ready to serve.

★ ★ ★

TOO EASY CHOCOLATE CAKE

Serves 12

Though he has had a long and admirable career, Doug Flutie will forever be known for the miraculous completion he made for Boston College back in 1984 to beat Bernie Kosar and the University of Miami. In the same spirit, you might work your tail off making an admirable spread, but all anyone will be talking about is this cake, which you just threw together.

Unsweetened cocoa powder for dusting pan
1 box (20 ounces) chocolate cake mix
1 box (2¾ ounces) chocolate pudding mix
16 ounces sour cream
2 eggs
12 ounces semisweet chocolate chips or mint chocolate chips

At home Preheat the oven to 350°F. Lightly butter a Bundt pan and dust with cocoa powder.

In a large bowl, whisk together the cake and pudding mixes.

In a small bowl, whisk together the sour cream and eggs. Stir in the chocolate chips.

Add the wet ingredients to the dry mixture and stir together until combined.

Transfer the batter to the Bundt pan and bang it gently on the counter a couple of times to settle the batter evenly.

Bake on the center rack of the oven until a toothpick inserted in the center comes out clean, about 50 minutes.

Transfer the pan to a wire rack and let cool. Run a knife around the edge of the cake, then invert the cake onto a platter. Clean and dry the Bundt pan and return the cake to the pan. Cover with aluminum foil and keep refrigerated until you are ready to pack, up to 24 hours.

At the tailgate Invert the cake onto a platter and cut into slices.

Note You need to bake this cake in a Bundt pan. You may have a signed Joe Namath rookie card, but there's a good chance you don't own a Bundt pan. They're not hard to come by. Just go to any housewares department, and look under "B" for Bundt pan.

★ ★ ★

IDEAL CHOCOLATE CAKE

Serves 12

The "Who was the greatest running back after Jim Brown?" debate will never be answered to anyone's satisfaction. Some tout Walter "Can't-Say-a-Bad-Word-about-Him" Payton. Others, quietly, are still loyal to O.J. "Dare-We-Even-Speak-His-Name" Simpson. There are the Gayle "What-Might-Have-Been" Sayers supporters. And then there are the Emmit "Overrated!/Underrated!" Smith fans. But one topic at your tailgate that will not be under debate is whether anyone has ever tasted a better chocolate cake than this one.

- **¼ cup unsweetened cocoa powder, plus more for dusting pan**
- **12 large eggs**
- **1 pound bittersweet chocolate**
- **2 cups granulated sugar**
- **1½ cups (3 sticks) butter, at room temperature**
- **1 cup all-purpose unbleached flour**
- **1 tablespoon powdered sugar**

At home Preheat the oven to 325°F. Lightly butter a 10-inch springform pan and dust with cocoa powder.

Separate the eggs, placing the yolks in a large bowl, the whites in a medium bowl.

Melt the chocolate on top of a double boiler, stirring occasionally. When completely melted, set aside to cool.

Add the granulated sugar to the bowl with the egg yolks and beat until the mixture is creamy and turns pale yellow, about 5 minutes. Add the butter and fold until just combined. Add the cooled chocolate and fold until just combined. Fold in the flour and ¼ cup cocoa powder.

Beat the egg whites until soft peaks form. Stir one-fourth of the egg whites into the chocolate batter to lighten it, then fold in the remaining egg whites.

Transfer the batter to the prepared pan and bake on the center rack of the oven for 1 hour and 10 minutes. Insert a toothpick into the center. If it comes out with little crumbs attached, it's okay. If it is smeared with batter, let it bake for 5 minutes more and test again. The cake will be firm on top, but the center will be a little soft.

Transfer the cake to a wire rack and let cool for an hour before removing from the pan. Store in a sealable cake container, or wrap in plastic and return the cake to the pan for safekeeping. Refrigerate until you are ready to pack, up to 24 hours.

At the tailgate Dust the cake with the powdered sugar and serve.

★ ★ ★

LEMON-POPPYSEED POUND CAKE WITH BURNT BUTTER FROSTING

Serves 8

Besides deviled eggs, this pound cake with burnt butter frosting is another memory my friend Molly has from her family's tailgating in Minnesota. The browned butter adds a distinctive nuttiness to the frosting.

POUND CAKE

- **2½ cups unbleached all-purpose flour**
- **¼ cup cornstarch**
- **1 teaspoon baking powder**
- **1 teaspoon salt**
- **1¼ cups (2½ sticks) butter, at room temperature**
- **2 cups granulated sugar**
- **6 large eggs**
- **3 tablespoons poppyseeds**
- **3 tablespoons fresh lemon juice**
- **1 tablespoon vanilla extract**
- **1 tablespoon grated lemon zest**
- **1 cup milk**

BURNT BUTTER FROSTING

- **½ cup (1 stick) butter**
- **2 cups powdered sugar**
- **2 teaspoons vanilla extract**
- **2 tablespoons milk**

At home **For the pound cake:** Preheat the oven to 325°F. Butter a Bundt pan and lightly dust with flour.

In a medium bowl, whisk together the flour, cornstarch, baking powder, and salt.

In a large bowl, use an electric mixer or wooden spoon to beat the butter and granulated sugar until smooth and creamy. Beat in the eggs one at a time, until smooth. Add the poppyseeds, lemon juice, vanilla, and lemon zest.

Add half of the flour mixture followed by half of the milk and stir to combine. Add the remaining flour and milk and stir until just combined.

Transfer the batter to the prepared pan and bake on the center rack of the oven until a toothpick inserted in the center comes out clean, about 50 minutes. Let the cake cool in the pan for a few minutes, then run a small knife around the edge to separate the cake from the pan. Invert the cake onto a wire rack and gently remove the pan. Let the cake cool for 30 minutes before frosting.

For the burnt butter frosting: Melt the butter in a medium, heavy-bottomed pan over medium heat and cook until it just starts to turn golden brown, about 3 minutes. Add the powdered sugar gradually, stirring continuously. Add the vanilla and then the milk, 1 tablespoon at a time, until it is the consistency of frosting.

Spread the frosting over the top and sides of the cake and let cool. Transfer to a sealable cake container and refrigerate until you are ready to pack, up to 24 hours.

DRI
SMIRNOFF
GOVERNMENT WARNING: (1) ACCORDING TO THE SURGEON GENERAL, WOMEN SHOULD NOT DRINK ALCOHOLIC BEVERAGES DURING PREGNANCY BECAUSE OF THE RISK OF BIRTH DEFECTS. (2) CONSUMPTION OF ALCOHOLIC BEVERAGES IMPAIRS YOUR ABILITY TO DRIVE A CAR OR OPERATE MACHINERY AND MAY CAUSE HEALTH PROBLEMS.
DISTILLED FROM PREMIUM GRAIN
PRODUCED BY THE SMIRNOFF CO. STAMFORD, CT
WWW.SMIRNOFF.COM

NKS
J&B

For some, tailgate drinks are the real reason to freeze your tail off before the game. While I don't go that far, I do appreciate it when someone takes the time to make a special drink. It shows they care about their guests and that they don't mind working that extra little bit to make the meal complete. But while you are taking the trouble to carefully construct your Ginger Lemonade or daiquiris, just make sure you remembered to put the beer on ice.

★ ★ ★

CHERRY LIMEADE

Serves 4

A really refreshing drink—a little tart, a little sweet.

3 cups water

1 cup fresh lime juice (from about 6 large limes)

¼ cup cherry juice concentrate

¼ cup superfine sugar

At the tailgate Mix all the ingredients together in a pitcher. Add ice and serve.

Note Cherry concentrate is available in most health food stores.

GINGER LEMONADE

Serves 4

The ginger gives this lemonade a distinctive flavor—the perfect combination of tart and sweet, with just a little kick at the end.

GINGER SIMPLE SYRUP

1 cup sugar
1 cup water
4-inch piece fresh ginger, peeled and thinly sliced

1 cup fresh lemon juice (from about 6 medium lemons)
½ cup Ginger Simple Syrup
3 cups water

At home **For the ginger simple syrup:** In a medium saucepan, combine the sugar, water, and ginger in a medium saucepan and bring to a boil. Reduce the heat to low and simmer for 5 minutes. Strain the syrup into a heat-proof sealable bottle and let cool. Refrigerate until ready to use.

At the tailgate Mix the lemon juice, ginger syrup, and water together in a pitcher. Add ice and serve.

Note For a stronger ginger flavor, add more ginger when you're making the syrup.

HOT CHOCOLATE

Serves 4

Sometimes, when you're tailgating with the extended family and there seem to be more kids than adults around, you may have a yearning for a cup of hot chocolate instead of a cold beer. It's okay. Go ahead. No one will rat you out.

¼ cup sugar
¼ cup unsweetened cocoa powder
4 cups milk

At home In a small saucepan, combine the sugar, cocoa, and ½ cup of the milk and whisk over low heat until it becomes a smooth paste. Slowly pour in the rest of the milk. Raise the heat to medium and continue whisking until the mixture is well combined. Heat until hot, and pour into a thermos.

Note A thermos will keep drinks hot longer if you prime it first. Fill the container with boiling water and let it sit for a few minutes. Pour out the water and fill the thermos with whatever drink you're bringing with you.

★ ★ ★

HOT MULLED CIDER

Serves 6

Great for a cold day, especially when you know your team has no chance of winning and you're wondering why you're shivering in the parking lot when you could be home watching videos of last season.

- **4 cups apple cider**
- **1 lemon, thinly sliced**
- **1 orange, thinly sliced**
- **¼ teaspoon ground nutmeg**
- **¼ teaspoon ground cloves**
- **2 cinnamon sticks, 3 inches long, or ¾ teaspoon ground cinnamon**

At home or at the tailgate Combine all the ingredients in a medium saucepan over medium-high heat. When the cider is hot but not boiling, reduce the heat to low. Keep the cider hot for 30 minutes, making sure it doesn't come to a simmer.

Strain into an insulated container to keep hot.

Note You can mull the cider in a pot on the grill after all the cooking is done. Add a few more coals if needed to keep the cider hot.

MOJITO

Serves 1

The *mojito* is sort of a Cuban cousin to the traditional American mint julep. Ernest Hemingway is said to have enjoyed *mojitos*, but then there are few drinks he *didn't* enjoy. As refreshing as lemonade but with a bit of a kick, the *mojito* is the perfect drink to help you while away those hot summer days.

2 teaspoons superfine sugar
4 mint sprigs
Club soda
1 lime, cut in half
2 to 3 ounces light rum

At the tailgate Place the sugar, 3 sprigs of the mint, and a splash of club soda in a pint glass. Use the back of a spoon to lightly crush the mint, and stir to dissolve the sugar.

Squeeze both halves of the lime into the glass, leaving one juiced lime half in the mixture. Add the rum, stir, and then fill with ice. Top with more club soda, garnish with the remaining mint sprig, and serve.

★ ★ ★

FROZEN STRAWBERRY-MANGO DAIQUIRIS

Serves 4

You need a blender for these, of course. But owning a battery-operated blender becomes a more viable option every year as the quality improves and the prices come down. A quick search on the Web will yield a source for either the appropriate blender or a stocking big enough to hold one when you receive it ("Honey, how could you possibly have known I wanted this?!") next holiday season.

20 ice cubes
10 ounces rum
⅓ cup fresh lime juice (from 2 to 3 large limes)
2 ounces Triple Sec
½ mango, peeled, pitted, and cut into 1-inch pieces
½ cup fresh or frozen strawberries, hulled

At the tailgate Place the ice in the blender and pulse to crush it a bit. Add the rum, lime juice, Triple Sec, mango, and strawberries. Blend until smooth and serve.

★ ★ ★

SPRIGHTLY SANGRIA

Serves 8

As the NFL season starts earlier every year and sports pundits try to ascribe some semblance of meaning to preseason games, tailgaters are finding that they have need of cool drinks for those hot fall afternoons. This sangria solves that dilemma. It's not authentic (so don't invite your Catalan friends), but it sure is refreshing.

- **1 bottle dry red wine such as Merlot or Cabernet**
- **2 cinnamon sticks, 3 inches long**
- **1 cup fresh orange juice**
- **1 orange, thinly sliced and seeds removed**
- **¼ cup fresh lemon juice (from about 2 medium lemons)**
- **1 lemon, thinly sliced and seeds removed**
- **1 mango, peeled, pitted, and diced**
- **1 peach, pitted and cut into 1-inch pieces**
- **12 ounces Limonata (Italian lemon soda) or Sprite**

At the tailgate Mix together all the ingredients except the Limonata in a glass pitcher and let stand for 30 minutes at room temperature.

Add ice and the Limonata, mix together with a wooden spoon, and serve.

LONG ISLAND ICED TEA

Serves 2

When Barry Sanders ran the ball, he had a way of gliding effortlessly, as if he were going down a gentle hill in neutral. That is until someone tried to tackle him. It was only when the defender bounced off him like a leaf off a windshield that you realized the strength and power Sanders had. This drink is a lot like that, so don't be deceived.

- **1 ounce vodka**
- **1 ounce tequila**
- **1 ounce rum**
- **1 ounce gin**
- **1 ounce Triple Sec**
- **1½ ounces sour mix**
- **Cola**
- **2 lemon slices or 2 maraschino cherries for garnish**

At the tailgate Pour all the ingredients except the cola and garnish into a shaker and give one brisk shake. Divide the mixture betweeen 2 tall glasses filled with ice and add the cola to each. Garnish each drink with a slice of lemon or a maraschino cherry. Or both.

★ ★ ★

RUM ICED TEA

Serves 6

Here is a fun, potent cocktail that needs to be consumed attentively; otherwise you might find yourself alone in the parking lot singing "Day-O" while everyone else is in the stadium watching the game.

- **¼ cup sugar**
- **¼ cup water**
- **3 tablespoons fresh lemon juice**
- **1½ cups papaya or guava juice**
- **1 cup tea**
- **¾ cup dark rum**
- **½ teaspoon ground cinnamon**
- **6 mint sprigs for garnish**

At the tailgate Mix the sugar, water, lemon juice, papaya juice, tea, rum, and cinnamon together in a pitcher. Add lots of ice and divide among 6 glasses. Garnish each with a sprig of mint and serve.

★ ★ ★

FUZZY NAVELS

Serves 4

Not all tailgaters are buff jocks or formerly buff former jocks. Some are demure older women who remember watching players you have only heard about. Who knows, they may have even dated those players when they were at school together. Venerable tailgaters like these prefer to drink something with a little more charm than a bottle of beer. If one of these tailgating doyennes is part of your crowd, you might think of serving her a Fuzzy Navel, so named because . . . well, you decide.

6 ounces peach schnapps

2 cups fresh orange juice

4 orange slices for garnish

At the tailgate Mix the schnapps and orange juice together in a pitcher and fill with ice. Divide among 4 glasses, garnish each with a slice of orange, and serve.

BEER

Serves 1

Perhaps the favorite drink of tailgaters, beer is available in most supermarkets, package stores, grocery stores, party stores (both regular and drive-through), gas stations, department stores, and gourmet shops—pretty much anywhere except elementary schools and places of worship. Most tailgaters I know like to drink their beer cold. And often. Look for it in bottles, cans, and kegs, though some smaller breweries only bottle their beers. Remember, kegs require the proper tap equipment. A plastic hose is not going to work, no matter how hard you suck on it.

1 beer

At the tailgate Place the beer in some environment that will get it cold.

Once cold, open the beer, being careful not to shake it first.

Drink.

Note Most beer comes in easy-open pop-top cans or twist-off bottles. But some bottled beers do not have twist-off caps. These need to be identified before you attempt to open them. Trying to twist off a non-twist-off cap can be humiliating. You may want to pack a bottle opener, unless one of your kids has really strong teeth.

SPE
ME

CIAL

NIUS

Not every tailgate party needs to happen before the homecoming football game or the Daytona 500. There are plenty of other opportunities to tailgate that don't fit the norm. The only requirements are that an event of some significance is about to happen. You can tailgate waiting outside Madison Square Garden to buy Springsteen tickets; at your town's annual dog parade; or at a classic car show. I've included a few other events with appropriate menus. Feel free to invent your own occasions. The more tailgating, the better.

Fourth of July Parade

In Traverse City, Michigan, getting a prime seat for the annual Fourth of July parade is an important event. Although the crowd lining the route is rarely more than one deep, it is terribly important to be part of that first row. Where you sit on the route is also critical. For some, that means being close enough to their house to run a string of extension cords from the socket in the front hall to an electric griddle so they can cook up a steady stream of hot dogs and cherry brats all day long. For others, it's essential to be at the beginning of the parade route, before some of the more improvised floats start coming apart. And for a discerning few, the ideal place is at the tail end of the parade, so they can poke gentle fun at the hapless condition of the more improvised floats and laugh good-naturedly at their tuba-carrying friends, who are, by that point, clearly dragging their heels.

★ ★ ★

CHERRY CAPITAL COCKTAIL

Serves 2

Traverse City is known as the Cherry Capital of the world, so a cherry drink is in order. And after the fifth marching band, you'll be glad you had one of these cocktails. It will also allow you to view the local bakery's six-person walking French bread with the appropriate amount of whimsy.

1 ounce Campari
4 ounces vodka
2 ounces fresh orange juice
1 teaspoon cherry concentrate
Club soda
2 maraschino cherries

At the tailgate Mix together the Campari, vodka, orange juice, and cherry concentrate in a pitcher. Divide the mixture between 2 tall glasses filled with ice. Add a splash of club soda to each and garnish each drink with a maraschino cherry.

Note Cherry concentrate is available in most health food stores.

★ ★ ★

OVEN-FRIED CHICKEN DRUMSTICKS

Serves 6

As with *fried* fried chicken, do not store this in a sealed container or it will lose all its crispness well before the first cheerleader tosses her baton.

- ½ **cup plus 1 tablespoon salt**
- 6 **cups cold water**
- 4 **pounds chicken drumsticks**
- 3 **eggs**
- 1¼ **cups plain bread crumbs**
- 1 **tablespoon garlic powder**
- 1 **tablespoon dried basil**
- 1 **tablespoon ground black pepper**
- **Ketchup for serving**

At home Before cooking, in a large pot, stir the ½ cup salt into the water until the salt is dissolved. Add the drumsticks and let soak in the brine for at least 1 hour and up to 4 hours.

Preheat the oven to 375°F. Drain the drumsticks and pat them dry.

Beat the eggs in a wide, shallow bowl. Place the bread crumbs in a pie plate and mix in the remaining 1 tablespoon salt and the garlic powder, basil, and pepper.

Dip each drumstick in the egg and then into the bread crumb mixture, turning so they are entirely coated. Arrange the breaded drumsticks in an ungreased 11-by-17-inch baking pan so they are not touching.

Bake on the center rack of the oven until the drumsticks are golden brown and no longer pink in the center, 35 to 40 minutes. Let the chicken cool on a wire rack, then pack into a cardboard box or similar container and cover with a clean cloth.

At the tailgate Serve the chicken with ketchup, of course, and lots of napkins.

★ ★ ★

ALL-AMERICAN POTATO SALAD WITH BACON

Serves 6 to 8

Sometimes you just need potato salad. It's not fashionable. Sometimes it's not even edible. Overzealous moms smother it with way too much dressing. Prideful grandmas protect generations-old recipes that are curiously unpalatable. Nevertheless, if you're tailgating on the Fourth of July and you see that empty spot on your red-white-and-blue paper plate, you know that space can only be filled by a mound of all-American homemade potato salad.

3 pounds small red potatoes, cut in half
8 slices bacon, cooked until crisp and broken into ¼-inch pieces
1 medium red onion, finely chopped
3 stalks celery, cut into ½-inch pieces
3 hard-cooked eggs, coarsely diced
½ cup chopped fresh parsley
½ cup sour cream
½ cup mayonnaise
2 tablespoons cider vinegar
1 tablespoon Dijon mustard
Salt and ground black pepper
2 ounces potato chips, crumbled

At home Bring the potatoes to a boil in a large saucepan in enough cold water to cover by an inch. Reduce the heat to low and simmer until the potatoes are just cooked through, 16 to 18 minutes. (Remember, they'll cook a bit more after you remove them from the pot.) Drain well in a colander, transfer to a large mixing bowl, and let cool for about 20 minutes. Gently turn the potatoes with a rubber spatula to allow the ones on the bottom to cool as well.

Add the bacon, onion, celery, eggs, and parsley.

In a small bowl, combine the sour cream, mayonnaise, vinegar, mustard, and salt and pepper to taste. Stir to combine. Add the dressing to the potato mixture and gently mix together with a rubber spatula until well combined. Add more salt if needed. Transfer to a sealable container and refrigerate until you are ready to pack, up to 24 hours.

At the tailgate Top the potato salad with the potato chips and serve.

CUCUMBER SALAD

Serves 6

Cucumber salad fills out this patriotic meal. Kirby cucumbers work best here, as they maintain their crunchiness longer in the dressing.

- **1 pound Kirby (pickling) cucumbers, cut into ¼-inch rounds**
- **1 small red onion, cut in half lengthwise and then thinly sliced**
- **2 tablespoons chopped fresh dill**
- **¼ cup rice vinegar or white wine vinegar**
- **2 tablespoons fresh lemon juice**
- **2 tablespoons olive oil**
- **½ teaspoon salt**
- **½ teaspoon ground black pepper**

At home Put the cucumbers, onion, and dill in a medium bowl.

In a small bowl, whisk together the vinegar, lemon juice, olive oil, salt, and pepper and pour the dressing over the cucumber mixture. Transfer the salad to a sealable container and refrigerate for at least 1 hour before serving.

CHERRY PIE

Serves 8

Top with whipped cream and just a few blueberries for a patriotic motif.

- **4 cups frozen unsweetened tart cherries**
- **1 cup sugar**
- **3 tablespoons quick-cooking tapioca**
- **½ teaspoon almond extract**
- **2 purchased frozen 9-inch pie shells**
- **2 tablespoons butter**
- **1 can pressurized whipped cream (optional)**

At home Preheat the oven to 375°F.

In a large mixing bowl, combine the frozen cherries, sugar, tapioca, and almond extract and let the mixture sit for 15 minutes.

Using a slotted spoon, transfer the cherry mixture to one of the pie shells. Dot the filling with the butter. After it has thawed slightly, remove the second pie shell from its pan and set it on top of the pie to form the top crust. Crimp the edges of the pastry together and cut 3 slits in the top to let the steam escape.

Bake on the center rack of the oven until the top crust is lightly browned and the filling is bubbling, 50 to 55 minutes.

Transfer the pie to a wire rack and let cool. Store at room temperature for up to 24 hours, covered loosely with a clean kitchen cloth. Do not refrigerate.

At the tailgate Cut the pie into slices and serve topped with whipped cream, if desired.

Wake Up and Smell the Tailgating: A Breakfast Menu

Tailgating before a game with a noon start can sometimes be confounding. Your first impulse is to get out the grill and start rounding up all the usual culinary suspects. But hard as it is for a die-hard tailgater to admit, you may not be quite ready at 11 A.M. for brats or burgers or even a steak. Calmer, more friendly fare is sometimes called for. Yet your Y tailgating chromosome blanches at the idea of some kind of prissy food that smacks of doilies and mimosas. Here's a benevolent menu that still has enough vigor to it that it doesn't resonate too much with the stigma of brunch.

BLOODY MARYS

Serves 2

Everyone who likes Bloody Marys has their own way of preparing them. Providing some Worcestershire, Tabasco, and a small bowl of horseradish at your tailgate will allow your crew to doctor their drinks to their liking.

8 ounces tomato juice
2 ounces vodka
½ teaspoon prepared white horseradish
Dash of Worcestershire sauce
Dash of Tabasco sauce
2 celery sticks

At the tailgate In a small pitcher, mix together the tomato juice, vodka, horseradish, and Worcestershire and Tabasco sauces. Divide the mixture between 2 glasses filled with ice and garnish each with a celery stick.

SMOKED WHITEFISH SPREAD

Serves 8 to 10

Great with crackers, bagels, or a sliced baguette, this spread is a fine way to start a tailgating day.

- **1½ pounds smoked whitefish**
- **1 small red onion, grated**
- **½ cup finely chopped celery**
- **3 tablespoons sour cream**
- **1 tablespoon mayonnaise**
- **1 tablespoon fresh lemon juice**
- **Chopped chives or scallions for serving**

At home Carefully remove the meat from the whitefish, leaving behind the bones, and transfer to a medium bowl. Pick through the meat twice more to remove any bones that might have snuck in.

Add the onion, celery, sour cream, mayonnaise, and lemon juice, and mix together. Transfer the spread to a sealable container and refrigerate until ready to pack.

At the tailgate Garnish the spread with some chopped chives and serve.

★ ★ ★

MEXICAN FRITTATA

Serves 6

Don't let anyone tell you a frittata is like a quiche without a crust. It tastes better than a quiche and doesn't have any stigma attached to it.

- **1 dozen large eggs**
- **1 cup grated cheese, such as Cheddar or Gruyère**
- **2 tablespoons olive oil**
- **1 tablespoon butter**
- **4 ounces andouille or other smoked, spicy sausage, cut into ½-inch pieces**
- **1 medium onion, thinly sliced**
- **6 ounces button mushrooms, stems trimmed, sliced**
- **1 can (4 ounces) diced green chiles, drained**
- **6 ounces baby spinach leaves, washed**
- **1 cup Salsa Cruda (page 22) or other salsa**
- **1 cup sour cream**

At home Preheat the broiler and adjust the oven rack to the upper third of the oven.

In a medium bowl, beat the eggs. Add the cheese and stir to combine.

Place a 12-inch ovenproof skillet, preferably cast iron, over high heat, and let it get very hot, about 2 minutes. Add the olive oil and butter and spread them evenly over the pan. Add the sausage, onion, and mushrooms and cook until the vegetables soften, about 8 minutes. Add the chiles and spinach and cook until the spinach wilts, about 2 minutes more.

Pour the egg mixture into the pan and cook, stirring continuously, until the eggs are almost set. Use a metal spatula to scrape the eggs from the bottom of the pan and incorporate them into the mixture.

Transfer the pan to the oven and broil the frittata until the top is nicely browned, 3 to 5 minutes. Remove the frittata from the oven and let it rest in the pan for about 5 minutes.

Remove the frittata from the pan (remember that the handle is still hot) by running a metal spatula around the edge and sliding it halfway underneath the frittata to loosen it. Tilt the pan and use the spatula to ease the frittata out onto a serving platter. Wrap the warm frittata in aluminum foil for transporting to the tailgate.

At the tailgate Cut the frittata into 6 wedges and serve warm or at room temperature with the salsa and sour cream on the side.

★ ★ ★

SAUSAGE BALLS

Serves 8

This gem comes via Knoxville, Tennessee—Vol country—where they know there's no better way to start your day than with a sausage ball.

1 cup unbleached all-purpose flour
8 ounces sweet Italian bulk sausage
8 ounces ground pork
¼ cup chopped fresh parsley
¼ cup chopped fresh mint
2 tablespoons fennel seed
1 tablespoon grated orange zest
1 teaspoon ground black pepper
4 tablespoons olive oil

At home Line a sheet pan or large platter with wax paper. Measure the flour into a wide, shallow bowl or pie plate.

In a medium bowl, combine the sausage, pork, parsley, mint, fennel, orange zest, and pepper and mix well with your hands until combined. Shape the sausage mixture into balls about 1 inch in diameter (they will be slightly smaller than meatballs). Transfer the balls to the bowl with the flour and toss gently so they are dusted on all sides. Shake off the excess flour and transfer the balls to the wax paper.

Place a skillet, preferably cast iron, over high heat and let it get very hot, about 2 minutes. Add 2 tablespoons of the olive oil and spread it evenly over the pan. Add half the sausage balls and cook, shaking the pan gently so the balls cook on all sides, about 8 minutes. Transfer to paper towels to drain. Add the remaining 2 tablesoons olive oil and cook the remaining balls. Let cool, then transfer to a sealable container until you are ready to pack, up to 24 hours.

At the tailgate Serve the sausage balls hot (reheat in the skillet on the grill) or at room temperature, with toothpicks stuck in at a rakish angle.

★ ★ ★

SOUR CREAM COFFEE CAKE

Serves 12

You may make this coffee cake initially for a morning tailgate meal, but after that you'll see no reason why you couldn't serve it for dessert anytime, even when your team hosts Monday Night Football.

2 cups sugar
1 cup chopped walnuts
2 teaspoons ground cinnamon
2½ cups unbleached all-purpose flour
2 teaspoons baking powder
1 teaspoon baking soda
1 teaspoon salt
½ cup (1 stick) butter, at room temperature
3 large eggs
1 teaspoon vanilla extract
12 ounces sour cream

At home Preheat the oven to 350°F. Grease a Bundt pan and dust with flour.

In a small bowl, mix together ½ cup of the sugar, the walnuts, and cinnamon. Set aside.

In a medium bowl, whisk together the flour, baking powder, baking soda, and salt. Set aside.

In a large bowl, use an electric mixer or wooden spoon to beat together the butter with the remaining 1½ cups sugar until the mixture lightens in color and is somewhat fluffy, about 2 minutes. Add the eggs, one at a time, beating well after each egg. Stir in the vanilla.

With a wooden spoon, stir in half the sour cream. Add half the flour mixture and stir to incorporate. Stir in the remaining sour cream and then the remaining flour mixture.

Sprinkle one third of the walnut mixture on the bottom of the prepared pan. Top with one-third of the batter. Sprinkle another third of the walnut mixture over the batter and cover with another third of the batter. Sprinkle with the remaining walnut mixture and top with the remaining batter.

Gently tap the Bundt pan on the counter to settle the batter. Bake on the center rack of the oven until a toothpick inserted in the center comes out clean, about 1 hour and 10 minutes.

Transfer the cake to a wire rack and let cool for 20 minutes. Place a large plate over the top of the pan. Holding firmly to both the pan and the plate, invert them so the cake falls onto the plate. Set the plate on a work surface and lift off the pan.

Let cool for another 30 minutes. Transfer to a sealable cake container and refrigerate until you are ready to pack, up to 24 hours.

At the tailgate Cut into slices and serve.

A Tailgate Thanksgiving

This is when you know you've graduated to the upper echelon of tailgating. Instead of being all cozy in your den, leaning back in the La-Z-Boy, picking stuffing out of your teeth and wiping cranberry sauce off your shirt, you're on the front lines, in the tailgating trenches. But you feel no regrets. Perhaps it's your son's high school game, so you're set up on the edge of the field, keeping warm before kickoff. Or maybe you're outside an NFL stadium, partying with some other ultra-serious fans. Maybe next Thanksgiving you'll stay inside, but as the first snow falls and your son and the rest of his team run by on their way to the field, you know there's nowhere else you'd rather be.

★ ★ ★

GRILLED TURKEY FILLETS

Serves 6

No worrying about when to put the turkey in the oven or when to take it out when you cook it outside on the grill.

- **¼ cup olive oil**
- **¼ cup sherry**
- **¼ cup finely chopped shallot**
- **4 tablespoons finely chopped garlic**
- **6 turkey breast fillets (about 3½ pounds total), cut about 1 inch thick**
- **Salt and ground black pepper**

At the tailgate Prepare coals for a medium-hot fire.

While the coals are heating, mix together the olive oil, sherry, shallot, and garlic. When the coals are ready, arrange them so that one side of the grill is hot and the other side is medium. Brush each side of the turkey fillets with the olive oil mixture and season with salt and pepper.

Grill the fillets on the hot side of the grill until nicely browned, 2 to 3 minutes. Turn and grill for 2 to 3 minutes more. Shift the fillets to the medium side and grill, turning once and brushing with the olive oil mixture, until the turkey is just cooked through, 6 to 7 minutes more.

SAUSAGE AND APPLE STUFFING

Serves 6

Thanksgiving wouldn't be complete without it. Make this at home the day before and wrap it in foil.

8 ounces sweet Italian bulk sausage
1 tablespoon olive oil
1 medium onion, finely chopped
1 bulb fennel, cut into ½-inch pieces
1 tart apple, such as Granny Smith, peeled, cored, and cut into ½-inch pieces
6 cloves garlic, finely chopped
Salt and ground black pepper
¼ cup port or sherry
2 cups chicken broth
4 slices bread, cut into ¾-inch cubes

At home Place a skillet over high heat and let it get hot, about 2 minutes. Add the sausage and cook until it is no longer pink, about 8 minutes, breaking up the meat with the back of a spoon. Remove the sausage with a slotted spoon and transfer to a platter.

Pour out the grease and return the pan to the heat. Add the olive oil and spread it evenly over the pan. Add the onion and fennel and cook until they begin to soften, about 6 minutes. Add the apple and cook for 4 minutes more. Add the garlic, season with salt and pepper, and cook for 3 minutes more.

Add the port and boil until reduced by half. Add the chicken broth and bread cubes and cook, stirring often, until the liquid is almost all gone, about 5 minutes.

Transfer the stuffing to a bowl and let it cool.

Cut three 16-inch pieces of aluminum foil. When the stuffing is cool enough to handle, divide it evenly among the foil pieces. Bring the long ends of the foil together and fold them tightly several times. Then fold up the sides to make a neat, sealed packet.

At the tailgate Arrange the foil packets around the edge of the grill while cooking the turkey. Turn them whenever you turn the turkey fillets. Open the packets carefully to avoid the escaping steam, transfer the stuffing to a platter, and serve.

CRANBERRY SAUCE

Makes about 2 cups

One of the jobs during a NASCAR pit stop is to catch any excess gas that might spill while the Gas Man is dumping it into the car. The person who does this is called the Gas Catch Man. It's a little thing, but it's a critical part of the pit stop. Kind of the way cranberry sauce is to Thanksgiving.

4 cups (about 1 pound) fresh cranberries
½ cup sugar
12 grapes, cut in half lengthwise
2 tablespoons fresh lime juice

At home Place all the ingredients in a medium saucepan over medium heat. Cover the pan and cook, stirring occasionally, until the cranberries soften and break open, about 15 minutes.

Remove the cranberries and grapes with a slotted spoon and transfer to a medium bowl. Continue cooking the liquid, uncovered, until it is reduced by half, then add it to the bowl with the cranberries. Let cool, transfer to a sealable container, and refrigerate for up to 5 days.

★ ★ ★

BAKED POTATO AND ONION

Serves 6

These are even better than the baked potatoes that come out of your oven at home.

6 baking potatoes, washed and dried
Salt and ground black pepper
2 medium onions, cut in half lengthwise and then into ¼-inch slices
6 cloves garlic, thinly sliced
2 teaspoons dried thyme

At home Cut each potato crosswise into 4 slices. Lay the slices flat on a work surface, keeping them oriented in their original positions. Season the tops well with salt and pepper.

Place 1 slice of onion and a few slices of garlic over each slice of potato. Season lightly with the thyme. Reassemble the potatoes into their original shapes and wrap in a double layer of aluminum foil.

At the tailgate Bake the potatoes in the foil by placing them among the coals as soon as you spread them over the bottom of the grill. Cook for 18 minutes, which means they will come out just when you have the rest of the meal assembled.

Unwrap carefully to avoid the escaping steam, and serve. The potatoes will be very hot for several minutes, so make your guests aware of this.

Note Either the Green Beans with Horseradish Sauce (page 190) or Grilled Asparagus (page 192) would go great with this Thanksgiving meal.

APPLE CRISP

Serves 6

Here's the real way to cap off Thanksgiving dinner. Or any meal.

- **6 cups peeled, cored, and sliced apples**
- **2 tablespoons sugar**
- **1 teaspoon ground cinnamon**
- **Pinch ground nutmeg, preferably freshly grated**
- **2 tablespoons fresh lemon juice**
- **½ cup packed brown sugar**
- **6 tablespoons (¾ stick) cold butter, cut in half lengthwise and then into ¼-inch slices**
- **½ cup rolled oats**
- **½ cup unbleached all-purpose flour**
- **½ cup walnuts**
- **Dash of salt**

At home Preheat the oven to 400°F. Lightly grease an 8-inch square baking pan.

Place the apple slices in a large bowl, add the sugar, ½ teaspoon of the cinnamon, the nutmeg, and lemon juice and mix so the apple slices are coated.

Place the brown sugar, butter, oats, flour, walnuts, salt, and the remaining ½ teaspoon cinnamon in the bowl of a food processor fitted with a steel blade and pulse a few times until everything is mixed together.

Arrange the apples in the prepared baking pan. Crumble the topping in an even layer over the apples and bake on the center rack of the oven until the topping is lightly browned, 35 to 40 minutes. Transfer the apple crisp to a wire rack and let cool.

Note Because the crisp is such a snap to prepare, try to bake it the morning of the meal. You can assemble the topping the night before. Do not wrap the crisp in plastic, as it will make the topping soggy. Instead, cover it with a clean kitchen cloth. By the time you're ready to serve the crisp, the coals will have died down enough that you can place the crisp in the closed grill for a few minutes to warm it up.

Football Style

The following football-shaped dishes will add a bit of jollity to your tailgate party, especially if you're partying at a baseball game. The recipes embrace the football motif in a variety of ways.

PIGSKIN MEXICAN DIP

Serves 12 as an appetizer

The good ol' football-shaped chopped liver mold with the pimiento and diced egg white laces has officially gone the way of the Nash Rambler and the hour-long network evening news. It's "Goodnight, Chet" to the chopped liver and *buenos días* to this more flavorful dip.

Romaine lettuce leaves or green kale for serving
8 ounces cream cheese
2 cups grated Cheddar cheese, plus a 2-ounce piece cut into 4-by-½-inch strips for serving
1 cup refried beans
1 can (4 ounces) diced green chiles, drained
1 tablespoon chili powder
1 teaspoon ground cumin
1 teaspoon salt
Tortilla chips for serving

At home Line a platter with the lettuce leaves.

In a medium bowl, use your hands to mix together the cream cheese, 2 cups Cheddar cheese, refried beans, chiles, chili powder, cumin, and salt until they are well combined. Place the mixture in the center of the platter. Shape it into something resembling a football. Smooth with a rubber spatula.

Arrange the strips of Cheddar along the top to make the laces. Transfer carefully to a really big sealable container or a cardboard box and refrigerate until you are ready to pack, up to 8 hours.

At the tailgate Serve the dip with chips and a whistle.

★ ★ ★

CHOCOLATE SHORTBREAD FOOTBALL COOKIES

Makes about 2 dozen cookies

Having a football-shaped cookie cutter makes these cookies a "snap." Your friends will be in motion to huddle around and maintain possession of them.

- 1 cup (2 sticks) butter, at room temperature
- ¾ cup granulated sugar
- 1 egg yolk
- 1¾ cups unbleached all-purpose flour
- ½ cup unsweetened cocoa powder
- ¼ cup cornstarch
- Pinch of salt
- 2 tablespoons milk
- ½ cup powdered sugar

At home In a bowl, using an electric mixer or wooden spoon, beat the butter and granulated sugar until well combined, about 1 minute. Add the egg yolk and mix for another minute.

Add the flour, cocoa powder, cornstarch, and salt, and mix until the dough holds together. This will take a minute or so. The dough will be stiff but pliable.

Transfer the dough to a large piece of plastic wrap or a work surface and use your palm to flatten the dough into a rough disk shape (this will make it easier to roll out later). Wrap the disk in the plastic and refrigerate until firm, at least 45 minutes (the dough must be cold to hold its shape).

Preheat the oven to 275°F.

Remove the dough from the plastic wrap and roll out on a lightly floured work surface until it is ½ inch thick. Cut the cookies into football shapes with a cookie cutter or freehand with a knife and transfer them to an ungreased baking sheet.

Bake on the center rack of the oven until the cookies are baked through but still soft, 25 to 30 minutes. Let them cool on the baking sheet before gently transferring them to a wire rack to cool completely.

In a medium bowl, mix the milk and powdered sugar together to form a thick but spreadable icing. Transfer to a small, resealable bag. Cut a ⅛-inch piece off one of the bottom corners and use the bag as a piping bag to decorate the cookies with football laces. Remember to shape them in a slight curve to simulate the roundness of the ball. Transfer to a sealable container, separating layers of cookies with wax paper. Store at room temperature until packing.

49ERS
WISTROM
96

★ ★ ★

TEAM CAKE

Serves 12 to 16

Remember, it isn't always the guy with the biggest steak who is the most ardent tailgater. Look for a party that has a cake decorated in their team's colors. There you'll find a true expression of the tailgating spirit.

2¾ cups unbleached all-purpose flour
1½ tablespoons baking powder
1 teaspoon salt
¾ cup (1½ sticks) butter, at room temperature
1¾ cups sugar
5 eggs
1 egg yolk
2 teaspoons vanilla extract, or 1 tablespoon orange juice and 2 tablespoons grated orange zest
1 cup milk
1 pound sweetened flaked coconut
4 drops green food coloring
2 jars (12 ounces each) white frosting
Assorted food coloring
1 tube (3 ounces) decorative white icing
3 drinking straws

At home Preheat the oven to 350°F. Butter an 11-by-17-inch sheet pan and dust lightly with flour.

In a medium bowl, whisk together the flour, baking powder, and salt.

In a large bowl, use an electric mixer or wooden spoon to beat the butter and sugar until smooth and creamy. Beat in the eggs and egg yolk, one at a time, until smooth. Add the vanilla or orange juice and orange zest.

Add half of the flour mixture, followed by half of the milk, and stir to combine. Add the remaining flour and milk and stir until just combined.

Transfer the batter to the prepared pan and bake on the center rack of the oven until a toothpick inserted in the center comes out clean, about 25 minutes. Let the cake cool in the pan for a few minutes, then run a knife around the edge and invert the pan over a wire rack to remove the cake. Let it cool completely before decorating.

Cut two 12-by-18-inch pieces of cardboard, stack them together, and wrap them with a single layer of aluminum foil. This will be the base for the cake.

Place the coconut in a resealable plastic bag. Add the green food coloring, seal the bag, and shake and massage the food coloring into the coconut until it is completely colored.

Cover the cake with the white frosting, reserving ½ cup. Mix food coloring into the reserved frosting to make it your team's colors. Frost 1½ inches at each end of the cake to depict the end zone.

Use the tube of icing to write the name of your team in white over the color at the end zone. Sprinkle the green coconut evenly over the center of the cake to make the field.

Draw 20 lines across the cake with the white icing to make the yardage lines on the field. Add the yardage numbers if you like.

Use the straws and some tape to make an old-fashioned H-shaped goal post. Set this in the back of the end zone.

Transport the cake carefully to the tailgate, even if it means someone has to take a bus to get to the party.

INDEX

-T-

-V-

-W-

-Z-

TABLE OF EQUIVALENTS

The exact equivalents in the following tables have been rounded for convenience.

Liquid/Dry Measures

U.S.	Metric
¼ teaspoon	1.25 milliliters
½ teaspoon	2.5 milliliters
1 teaspoon	5 milliliters
1 tablespoon (3 teaspoons)	15 milliliters
1 fluid ounce (2 tablespoons)	30 milliliters
¼ cup	60 milliliters
⅓ cup	80 milliliters
½ cup	120 milliliters
1 cup	240 milliliters
1 pint (2 cups)	480 milliliters
1 quart (4 cups, 32 ounces)	960 milliliters
1 gallon (4 quarts)	3.84 liters
1 ounce (by weight)	28 grams
1 pound	454 grams
2.2 pounds	1 kilogram

Length

U.S.	Metric
1/8 inch	3 millimeters
¼ inch	6 millimeters
½ inch	12 millimeters
1 inch	2.5 centimeters

Oven Temperature

Fahrenheit	Celsius	Gas
250	120	½
275	140	1
300	150	2
325	160	3
350	180	4
375	190	5
400	200	6
425	220	7
450	230	8
475	240	9
500	260	10